Preserving with
Aunt Daisy

PRESERVING WITH
Aunt Daisy

Over 200 trusted recipes for
jams, jellies, pickles and chutneys

Hodder Moa

National Library of New Zealand Cataloguing-in-Publication Data
Daisy, Aunt, 1879-1963.
Preserving with Aunt Daisy : over 200 trusted recipes for jams, jellies,
pickles and chutneys / editor, Barbara Basham.
Includes index.
ISBN 978-1-86971-306-5
1. Condiments. 2. Canning and preserving. I. Basham, Barbara. II. Title.
641.852—dc 23

A Hodder Moa Book
Published in 2013 by Hachette New Zealand Ltd
4 Whetu Place, Mairangi Bay
Auckland, New Zealand
www.hachette.co.nz

Text © Estate of Barbara Basham 2013
The moral rights of the author have been asserted.
Design and format © Hachette New Zealand Ltd 2013

All rights reserved. No part of this publication may be reproduced or transmitted in any form or by any means, electronic or mechanical, including photocopying, recording, or any information storage and retrieval system, without permission in writing from the publisher.

Photographs by Simon Young
Food styling by Pippa Cuthbert
Designed and produced by Hachette New Zealand Ltd
Printed by Everbest Printing Co Ltd

Contents

Preface	7
About *Preserving with Aunt Daisy*	9
Measurements	9
Cooking Instructions	10
Ingredients	10
The Preserving Process	12
Equipment	14
Straining (for jelly-making only)	15
Sterilising Jars	16
The Seasons	17
Chutneys & Relishes	19
Pickles	37
Sauces & Ketchups	57
Jams & Jellies	65
Preserving	119
Recipe Index	140

PREFACE

This heritage collection of well-loved, tried and true Aunt Daisy recipes was originally read over ZB radio to housewives, mothers and cooks all over New Zealand from the 1930s to the 1960s.

Armed with pen and paper, many of our grandparents waited eagerly by the wireless to scribble down the latest great recipe for a succulent roast meal, a really good pavlova, or a moist golden syrup pudding to impress their families and friends. They knew that, with Aunt Daisy testing every recipe, they could be counted on to work.

It was a different time and, many will argue, a different world, but this is the kind of food most of us love to remember. It's comfort food in the best sense — wholesome, nutritious, and with a taste that never fails to make us recall the best family dinners.

Aunt Daisy's late daughter Barbara Basham lovingly researched and compiled this extensive collection as a tribute to her mother. Before Barbara died, she arranged to establish a charitable trust under her Will to which all sale proceeds from this book will go.

The Barbara Basham Medical Charitable Trust is managed by Guardian Trust to fund world-class medical research in New Zealand. The Trust recently provided funding to the Gillies McIndoe Research Institute to support the extraordinary work that has been undertaken by Professor Swee Tan and his team on strawberry birthmarks.

If you would like to support the Barbara Basham Medical Charitable Trust in this aim, donations are tax-deductible and can be made at any branch of Guardian Trust, or by cheque (payable to the Barbara Basham Medical Charitable Trust) to P O Box 913, Wellington. Donations to the Gillies McIndoe Research Institute may be made to P O Box 7184, Newtown Wellington.

We hope you and your family enjoy these recipes that little bit more, knowing that the sale proceeds of this collection will fund ongoing medical research in New Zealand.

Guardian Trust
THE TRUST COMPANY

ABOUT *PRESERVING WITH AUNT DAISY*

Recipes in *Preserving with Aunt Daisy* come from *The Aunt Daisy Cookbook*, which is one of New Zealand's bestselling recipe books. It was first published in 1968. Although Aunt Daisy's recipes themselves stand the test of time, some measurements and methods have changed over the years.

MEASUREMENTS

All recipes have been metricated. Pounds and ounces have been changed to grams, quarts and pints to millilitres, and inches to centimetres.

Breakfast cup and teacup measures remain unchanged. A breakfast cup is a little larger than a standard cup; about 280ml or ½ pint. A teacup is smaller than a standard cup; about 140ml or ¼ pint (similar to 1 gill). A rough conversion is:

1 breakfast cup = 1 standard cup + 2 tablespoons
1 teacup = ½ standard cup + 1 tablespoon
1 breakfast cup of sugar = 250g, 1 teacup of sugar = 125g

COOKING INSTRUCTIONS

Most of Aunt Daisy's recipes presumed the cook had a good amount of know-how. In the case of her preserving recipes, she presumed that every home cook was very familiar with sterilising jars and the process of bottling. Of course, this is not the case in this day and age when most canned and bottled products are bought at the supermarket. So before using Aunt Daisy's recipes, please read carefully the instructions below. Her tips on pages 20 and 66 are also useful.

NOTE: Aunt Daisy's recipes sometimes make large quantities. Adjust the recipe to your desired quantity. For example, if you want to use 2kg of fruit instead of 4kg make sure you halve all other ingredient quantities in the recipe.

INGREDIENTS

Below is a list of fruits used in some of Aunt Daisy's recipes that are not commonly available from supermarkets. These fruits are sometimes grown in home gardens and are occasionally available at farmer's markets in the right season.

CAPE GOOSEBERRY: A small round orange/yellow berry. On the bush it is encased in a papery lantern-like pod. Ripening through summer and autumn.

CHOKO: Green and pear-shaped, chokos grow on a vine. Usually available in April/May.

CRAB APPLE: Tiny red, very tart apples. Available autumn and winter.

DAMSON: A small dark purple plum with an astringent taste.

ELDERBERRY: Small red or blue/black berries. Ripe in summer.

GOOSEBERRY: A tart green berry — these days not as readily available as it once was. Fruiting in summer.

HAWTHORN BERRY: Small round red or red/purple fruit.
JAPONICA: A yellow apple-like fruit related to quince. Ripening in autumn.
LAURELBERRY: The fruit of the laurel tree — a small, shiny black berry.
LOGANBERRY: A cross between a raspberry and a blackberry. Ripe in summer.
MEDLAR: The fruit is brown, apple-shaped and hard. They ripen in late autumn.
MULBERRY: Red or black fruit of the mulberry tree. Ripe in autumn.
PIE MELON: The fruit looks like a watermelon, but the flesh is white and is not sweet. Available in autumn.
QUINCE: A yellow pear-like fruit. Ripens in autumn and early winter.

Also note the following:
CAYENNE PEPPER: Beware! The cayenne pepper used in Aunt Daisy's day was not as hot as that currently available. Please reduce the amount of cayenne pepper to taste.
MACE: This spice is commonly used in preserves but is becoming increasingly difficult to find in supermarkets. It is still readily available at specialist spice shops.
MUSHROOMS: Aunt Daisy often specifies 'freshly picked' which have a high water content. If using shop-bought mushrooms to make ketchup, use double the quantity. (Note: 1kg shop-bought portobello mushrooms makes ½ cup ketchup.)
PRESERVED GINGER: This usually meant ginger preserved in syrup, which is difficult to source these days. Substitute for crystallised ginger in sweet recipes or fresh ginger in others.
SALTPETRE: This is the mineral form of potassium nitrate, a common ingredient in salted meat. Curing salts are available from specialist shops or ask your butcher. It is not necessary to use saltpetre; its main role is to keep preserved meat a nice pink colour.

THE PRESERVING PROCESS

1. Get ready. Read the recipe carefully, making sure you have given yourself enough time (some recipes require prepared fruit or vegetables to be left overnight) and that you have all the required equipment (see Equipment list below). Assemble the ingredients.

2. Prepare fruit or vegetables. When selecting, remember that ripe is best unless specified otherwise in the recipe. Over-ripe or under-ripe fruit and veg will affect the final product. Wash and dry thoroughly, then peel, chop, grate, etc, as required.

3. Cooking. Following the recipe, place all the ingredients in your preserving pan and bring to the boil. For jelly-making, an extra step: straining, is required before adding the sugar and boiling again. This is explained in detail below.

4. Get ready again. Once you have followed the recipe and have a bubbling preserving pan on the cook top, take time to prepare for the next step. Sterilise your jars (see instructions below)

and have them ready. Consider how you are going to get your preserve from the pan and into the jars and get ready equipment needed such as funnel, small jug, ladle, etc. Have tea towels, an oven glove, or tongs nearby for handling hot jars.

5. The Setting Test. For jams and jellies you need to be sure that when you remove the mixture from the pan it will set. To do this, use the Setting Test. Put a little of the mixture on a cold plate and leave to cool for a minute. If the jam/jelly is ready this mixture will wrinkle when you touch it and a channel will remain in the centre when you draw your finger through it (i.e. the mixture does not join back together).

6. Fill jars. Place the hot, sterilised jars on a non-slip surface. Lift the hot preserve from the pan using a large ladle or a small jug and fill the jars. Be careful not to burn yourself. Do not fill the jars too full. NEVER fill cold jars with hot liquid.

7. Seal jars. Place the lids on the jars and loosely screw on. You will often hear a popping noise when the jar seals. Leave to cool completely before moving. For jars without lids, you can use a cellophane cover. Wet one side of the cellophane and place on top of the jar (wet side up). Secure with a rubber band. As the cellophane dries it will make a tight seal.

8. Store jars. It is a good idea to label jars before storing, so that you can remember what's in them and when it was made. Jars should always be stored in a cool, dark place. Remember the bottom of a cupboard tends to be cooler than the top.

EQUIPMENT

PRESERVING PAN — This is essential. A large saucepan will suffice if you are only making small quantities. (Note: brass and copper pans should not be used as they react with vinegar.)

MEASURING EQUIPMENT — It is essential to have accurate kitchen scales. You will also need a measuring jug and spoon measures.

GRATER — For flavourings such as lemon, ginger, nutmeg, etc.

SPOONS — A wooden spoon for stirring. A slotted metal spoon for removing scum is sometimes useful.

STRAINER FOR JELLY-MAKING — Special jelly bags and straining kits are available, but a piece of muslin or other fine cloth will do nicely. Make sure they have been boiled to sterilise then completely dried before use.

JAM FUNNEL — This is useful for filling jars and reducing mess, but it's by no means necessary.

SMALL JUG OR MUG — Many find that lifting hot liquid from the preserving pan in a small jug and filling jars with this is a good option.

JARS AND LIDS — Glass jars with metal plastic-lined lids are best (the plastic lining prevents the metal lid from reacting with the vinegar in pickles, etc, and makes a good seal).

CELLOPHANE AND RUBBER BANDS — If your glass jars have no lids, they can be covered with cellophane circles and secured with rubber bands.

STRAINING (FOR JELLY-MAKING ONLY)

If you are using a length of muslin or fine cloth to strain the boiled pulp, the easiest way is to use an inverted chair or stool. Securely attach a corner of the material to each leg of the chair, so that the material hangs in the centre, creating a 'straining bag'. (Ensure it will not hang too low when weighed down by the pulp, and that your bowl will comfortably fit under it.)

Place a large bowl under the strainer and pour in the cooled pulp. Leave to strain overnight. Don't squeeze to speed up the process — this could result in a cloudy jelly.

If you have a straining kit, place the jelly bag inside the metal stand and secure. Continue as above.

STERILISING JARS

All jars you are using must be thoroughly sterilised and kept warm. If not properly sterilised, you run the risk of your preserve going off. There are two common methods of sterilising:

OVEN METHOD
Wash all your jars and lids in hot soapy water. Rinse them thoroughly in hot water then place in an oven which has been pre-heated to 120°C. Leave them in the oven for 30 minutes. Remove using tongs or an oven glove.

BOILING METHOD
Boil jars and lids in a large pan of water for 15 minutes. Then leave them in the hot water until you are ready to use them. Remove using tongs and allow to dry just before filling.

THE SEASONS

In Aunt Daisy's heyday all cooking was seasonal as most fruit and vegetables were unavailable outside of their growing season. Today many fruits and vegetables are available in supermarkets and specialty shops all year round. However, this book will be of most use to those who wish to preserve what is in their garden or the fruits and vegetables that are good, plentiful and cheap in shops and markets. The table below is a basic guide to what is in season when. Remember that growing seasons vary slightly throughout the country.

Season	Fruit	Vegetable
Summer	Apricots, Blackberries, Blueberries, Cherries, Melons, Nectarines, Peaches, Plums, Raspberries, Strawberries	Beans, Beetroot, Capsicum, Courgettes, Cucumber, Squash, Sweetcorn, Tomatoes
Autumn	Apples, Feijoas, Mandarins, Pears, Plums, Tamarillos	Beetroot, Capsicum, Celery, Chokos, Pumpkin, Red Cabbage, Tomatoes
Winter	Grapefruit, Kiwifruit, Lemons, Mandarins, Oranges, Tangelos	Broccoli, Cauliflower, Leeks, Savoy cabbage
Spring	Apples, Lemons, Oranges, Rhubarb, Tangelos	Asparagus, Broad beans

Chutneys & Relishes

AUNT DAISY'S TIPS FOR SUCCESSFUL CHUTNEYS, PICKLES & SAUCES

- It is always desirable to put in a little less salt and mustard than stated until you taste the mixture. It is easy to add more seasoning, but impossible to take out once added.

- To prevent home-made pickles from shrinking, cover with wax after bottling.

- If pickles become shrunk and crusted, mix equal parts boiling water and vinegar, and a little sugar. Put on top of chutney. Do not take the dry crusty part off, but push it down in several places with a wooden skewer, and leave it for a while. Every now and then stir with the skewer. It should be as good as new.

Bean Relish, page 22

Beetroot Relish (Uncooked), page 23

APPLE CHUTNEY

900g tomatoes
1.8kg apples
2 large onions
450g sugar
60g salt
15g ground ginger
¼ teaspoon cayenne pepper
7g allspice
4 cups vinegar
450g raisins

Skin tomatoes, mince apples and peel onions.
Tie spices in a muslin bag. Boil all together in a saucepan for 1 or more hours, until brown and cooked.
Half a cup of finely chopped mint leaves added makes an interesting flavour.

APRICOT CHUTNEY

2.7kg apricots
1.2kg onions
790g sugar
1 dessertspoon salt
1 teaspoon cloves
1 teaspoon peppercorns
1 teaspoon ground mace
1 teaspoon curry powder
½ teaspoon cayenne pepper
4 cups vinegar

Cut up apricots and onions.
Put in a pan with the remaining ingredients.
Boil for 1 hour.
Nice in sandwiches for supper.

BEAN RELISH

12 cups vinegar
2 tablespoons salt
2 small teaspoons pepper
3 cups sugar
1.8kg sliced beans (scarlet runners are good)
7 large onions, finely sliced
2 tablespoons flour
2 tablespoons mustard
2 heaped teaspoons turmeric
a little cold water

Boil vinegar, salt, pepper, sugar, beans and onions together for 1 hour, or until tender.
Mix flour, mustard and turmeric with water. Stir into beans and boil a few minutes longer.
Cover when cold.
A small piece of finely chopped garlic is an improvement.

BEETROOT CHUTNEY

1.4kg beetroot
680g apples
2 onions
2 cups vinegar
½ teaspoon ginger
1 teaspoon salt
juice of 1 lemon
340g sugar

Boil beetroot until tender.
Cut into cubes when cold.
Cut apples and onions small and boil for 20 minutes with vinegar and remaining ingredients.
Add to beetroot and boil another 15 minutes.

BEETROOT RELISH (Uncooked)

3 medium beets, washed, scraped and skinned
½ cup sugar
a little cinnamon
salt and pepper
1 cup vinegar
a few cloves

Grate beets on a carrot grater, more finely than a piece of horseradish.
Add sugar, cinnamon, and salt and pepper.
Boil vinegar with cloves, and strain.
When cold, mix with beets.
Leave about a week before using.

CHOKO CHUTNEY

10 large chokos
680g stoned dates
680g sugar
3 large cooking apples
1 onion
220g preserved ginger
85 to 115g salt
1 teaspoon cayenne pepper
450g sultanas
6 cups vinegar
450g raisins

Cut up chokos finely and leave overnight.
Next morning boil all ingredients together until tender.

CHOW CHOW

1.4kg beans	30g spice
1.4kg onions	30g peppercorns
3 or 4 cucumbers	85 to 115g mustard
220g salt	½ teaspoon cayenne
8 cups vinegar	1 tablespoon turmeric
450g brown sugar	4 tablespoons flour
30g cloves	

Cut up vegetables and sprinkle with salt. Stand overnight. Drain.
Add 5 cups of the vinegar and boil, only until vegetables are tender.
Add sugar and all spices.
Mix flour with remaining vinegar. Add to vegetables and boil until thick.
Bottle.

CUCUMBER RELISH

450g apples (peeled before weighing)
2 cups vinegar
450g sugar
30g salt
1 teaspoon pepper

680g onions
680g cucumbers (unpeeled), minced
1 dessertspoon curry powder
2 tablespoons turmeric

Mince apples and cook in vinegar.
When soft, add sugar, salt, pepper and onions. Cook until soft.
Add cucumber and curry powder. Boil about 5 minutes.
  To colour, add turmeric.

FIG CHUTNEY

680g fresh figs
80g dates
60g preserved ginger
2 cups vinegar
170g brown sugar

80g raisins
220g onions
½ teaspoon salt
¼ teaspoon cayenne pepper

Cut figs into rings. Cut dates and ginger into cubes.
Boil vinegar and sugar. Pour over all other ingredients.
Leave overnight. Next day boil until thick and dark, about
  3 hours.

FRUIT CHUTNEY (with Quinces)

450g tomatoes
450g apples
450g quinces
280g onions
220g raisins
110g preserved ginger
  (or bruised whole ginger)
220g brown sugar
30 to 60g salt
15g ground ginger
½ teaspoon cloves
½ teaspoon cayenne
  pepper
2 cups vinegar

Chop fruit and vegetables finely.
Boil all ingredients for 2 to 3 hours.

GREEN GOOSEBERRY CHUTNEY

900g green gooseberries
450g chopped prunes
450g raisins or sultanas
450g sliced onions
60g ground ginger
a good pinch cayenne
  pepper
1 small teaspoon salt
4 cups vinegar
450g brown sugar

Boil all ingredients except sugar until fruit is pulpy.
Add sugar. Stir until dissolved.
Boil 1 minute. Bottle.

INDIAN CHUTNEY (with Gooseberry)

900g green gooseberry pulp
450g sultanas
450g dates, cut small
2 cups vinegar
30g garlic cut small
450g brown sugar
450g white sugar
115g preserved ginger
2 teaspoons cayenne pepper
60g salt

Boil all ingredients together for 15 minutes.
Bottle in wide-mouthed jars.

MANGO CHUTNEY

2.25kg half-ripe mangoes
4 cups vinegar
2.25kg sugar
4 small red peppers
115g garlic
220g raisins
220g preserved ginger
1 tablespoon salt
2 tablespoons whole cloves

Peel mangoes and cut in slices 12mm thick and 25mm long.
Bring vinegar and sugar to the boil. Add other ingredients and cook until mangoes are transparent.
Put fruit in jars and pour syrup over.
Leftover syrup may be used to pickle fresh or canned peaches, pears or apricots.

MINT & APPLE CHUTNEY

2.25kg sugar
2.25kg skinned and chopped tomatoes
2.25kg finely chopped onions
2.25kg peeled and sliced apples
8 cups vinegar
900g raisins
pinch of cayenne pepper
4 tablespoons salt
3 tablespoons mustard
2 cups chopped mint

Have all ingredients well pressed down in a large pan. Simmer gently for about 45 minutes.

PEACH CHUTNEY

2.7kg peaches, stoned and cut up
vinegar
1.4kg brown sugar
2 tablespoons salt (or as desired)
1 small teaspoon cayenne pepper
60g garlic
10g whole ginger, bruised and put in a muslin bag
4 cups sultanas

Cover peaches with vinegar.
Add all other ingredients.
Boil all to pulp.

PEACH & PLUM CHUTNEY

900g ripe but firm
    peaches, stoned
900g ripe but firm
    plums, stoned
salt and pepper
4 cups vinegar

1 cup brown sugar
6 tablespoons preserved
    ginger
4 tablespoons cloves
1 cup finely cut-up onions

Put layers of fruit in a dish. Sprinkle with salt and pepper. Leave 24 hours.

Drain. Put fruit in a pan with vinegar, brown sugar, ginger, cloves and onions.

Boil slowly until peaches are tender. Strain through a sieve. Fill small jars and make airtight.

PICCALILLI

1.4kg prepared marrow	salt
450g (medium) cauliflower	8 cups vinegar
450g French or runner beans	50g mustard
220g onions	50g ground ginger
½ large or 1 small cucumber	15g turmeric
	30g flour
	170g sugar

Quantities of vegetables may be varied but should be a total weight of 2.7kg.

Cut prepared vegetables into uniform pieces. Sprinkle well with salt and leave for 24 hours.

Drain thoroughly. Mix a little vinegar with spices and flour.

Boil vegetables with remaining vinegar and the sugar for about 20 minutes.

Stir in flour and spices and boil for 3 minutes. Bottle and cover.

SWEET PICCALILLI

900g green tomatoes	10 cups vinegar
900g onions	2 cups sugar
900g green beans	1 cup flour
1 medium cauliflower	4 tablespoons mustard
6 small cucumbers	1 tablespoon turmeric
brine of 1 cup salt to 4 cups water	

Mango Chutney, page 27

Mint & Apple Chutney, page 28

Wipe vegetables and cut up neatly.
Cut cauliflower stalks and put in. Break cauliflower into little florets.
Put all vegetables in brine, cover, and leave 48 hours.
Bring to scalding point in brine. Strain carefully.
Pour on 8 cups vinegar and bring to the boil.
Mix up sugar, flour, mustard and turmeric with the remaining 2 cups vinegar, and add.
Cook 10 minutes more.

PLUM CHUTNEY

2.7kg plums
3 cups vinegar
1.4kg apples, peeled, cored and quartered
1.4kg onions, cut up fine
900g sugar
110g salt
1 level teaspoon pepper
1 level teaspoon mustard
small piece of garlic, cut finely
220g dates
220g raisins
220g preserved ginger, chopped
1 dessertspoon whole allspice
1 dessertspoon pickling spices

Boil plums in vinegar then put through a sieve.
Add apples, onions and other ingredients, with spices in a muslin bag.
Stir well, and boil for 2 hours. Remove spice bag before bottling.

QUICK CHUTNEY

3 tablespoons plum jam
1 tablespoon Worcestershire sauce
1 tablespoon vinegar
salt to taste

Mix all together. Then ready for use.

QUINCE CHUTNEY

6 large quinces
450g ripe tomatoes
900g apples
4 large onions
900g brown sugar
60g salt
30g ground ginger
6 chillies
¼ teaspoon cayenne pepper
1 teaspoon mustard
1 teaspoon curry powder
220g seeded raisins
about 6 cups vinegar

Peel and cut up quinces, tomatoes, apples and onions.
Add all other ingredients except vinegar.
Mix then cover with vinegar.
Boil slowly for 3 to 4 hours. Bottle while hot.

RHUBARB CHUTNEY

900g rhubarb
2 finely cut lemons
900g sugar
30g bruised whole ginger

Boil all together until thick and dark.
Remove ginger. Bottle.

RHUBARB RELISH

2 cups chopped rhubarb
2 cups sliced onion
1 cup vinegar
2 cups brown sugar
½ tablespoon salt
cinnamon
ginger
cayenne pepper

Mix all ingredients in an enamel saucepan.
Boil 20 to 30 minutes, or until a jam consistency.
Bottle and seal.

TAMARILLO CHUTNEY

1.4kg tamarillos, skinned and cut up
450g onions
680g apples
2 cups vinegar
1.1kg brown sugar
half a packet of mixed spice
1 tablespoon salt
¼ to ½ teaspoon cayenne pepper

Boil for about 1 hour. Will make about 2.5kg chutney.

TOMATO CHUTNEY (Red)

24 large ripe tomatoes
85g salt
6 good-sized tart apples
3 onions
rind of 1 lemon

5 cups vinegar
30g garlic
400g light brown sugar
60g ginger
170g finely cut raisins

Slice tomatoes, sprinkle with salt and leave to drain overnight.
Add apples, onions, lemon rind and vinegar.
Boil until tender and put through a colander.
Add remaining ingredients. Boil for 3 or 4 hours.

TOMATO RELISH (Quite Hot)

900g tomatoes
4 large onions
salt
2 cups vinegar
2 cups sugar

10 small chillies
1 tablespoon curry powder
1½ teaspoons mustard
2 tablespoons flour

Cut tomatoes and onions in slices. Sprinkle with salt and leave overnight.
Drain next day. Boil in vinegar for about 10 minutes.
Add sugar and chillies. Add other ingredients mixed to a paste with a little cold vinegar.
Boil for 1½ hours. Bottle while hot.

GREEN TOMATO CHUTNEY

1.4kg green tomatoes
2 small cucumbers
4 large apples
3 large onions
170g sultanas
450g brown sugar
2 tablespoons mustard
1½ teaspoons ground ginger
½ level teaspoon cayenne pepper (or to taste)
1½ tablespoons salt
a little more than 2 cups vinegar

Peel, slice and cut up all vegetables.
Put all ingredients in a pan and gradually bring to the boil. Simmer for 2 to 3 hours, stirring often. Seal in jars.

Pickles

BLACKBERRY PICKLE

2 cups blackberries
450g white sugar
1 cup vinegar
15g ground ginger
30g allspice

Steep blackberries and sugar for 12 hours.
Bring vinegar to the boil. Add blackberries and boil for 30 minutes.
When cold, add ginger and spice, and mix well.
Put in jars and cover.

CABBAGE PICKLE (Uncooked)

cabbage or cauliflower
salt
allspice
best vinegar

Cut up cabbage (or cauliflower), sprinkle with salt and leave overnight.
In morning wash off salt and drain for half a day.
Put into jars with allspice sprinkled on the bottom. Sprinkle allspice in the middle and on top.
Cover with vinegar, filling the jars.
Cover tightly and keep in a cool place.

RED CABBAGE PICKLE

1 fresh dry red cabbage, finely cut	30g peppercorns
salt	30g ginger
vinegar — to every 4 cups vinegar allow:	30g allspice
	1 tablespoon sugar

Bring cabbage to the boil.
Strain and press into jars.
Boil vinegar mixed with peppercorns, ginger, allspice and sugar.
Pour hot vinegar over cabbage.
Ready in a week.

CABBAGE PICKLE (white)

1 large white cabbage, finely cut	4 cups vinegar
4 large onions	1 cup flour
salt	1 cup sugar
	2 cups vinegar

Sprinkle cabbage and onion with salt and leave to stand 24 hours.
Drain water off and boil vegetables slowly for 15 minutes in 4 cups vinegar.
Mix flour, sugar and 2 cups vinegar. Add to vegetables and boil for 10 minutes.
Put in jars, and cover when cold.

CAPERS, PICKLED

capers	1 bay leaf
vinegar — to each 2 cups vinegar add:	2 whole peppercorns
	1 teaspoon brown sugar
1 teaspoon mace	

Pick capers when ripe. Put in the sun for 1 day to dry.
Put in large jars with vinegar and let stand 3 or 4 weeks.
Drain, and pack closely in jars.
Bring vinegar, mace, bay leaf, peppercorns and sugar to the boil. Strain, and fill jars.
Cover closely and store in a cool dark place.
Best kept 2 months before using.

CAULIFLOWER PICKLE

1 cauliflower, cut up fine	salt
4 large onions, cut fine	4 cups vinegar

Sprinkle vegetables with salt and leave overnight. Strain.
Boil for 20 minutes in vinegar.

Sweet Piccalilli, page 30

Red Cabbage Pickle, page 39

Thickening:
- ½ cup flour
- 1½ teacups golden syrup
- ½ tablespoon curry powder
- ½ tablespoon turmeric
- 2 dessertspoons mustard mixed with 2 cups vinegar

Heat all ingredients until thick. Stir in to vegetables. Boil all for 5 to 6 minutes. Bottle when cold.

CAULIFLOWER & PINEAPPLE PICKLE

- 1.4kg sliced onions
- 1 large cauliflower broken into little florets
- handful of salt
- vinegar
- 1 large tin pineapple, cut small
- ½ cup flour
- 1 tablespoon mustard
- 2 tablespoons curry powder

Sprinkle onions and cauliflower with salt and leave overnight.
Next day, strain, and cover with vinegar. Boil for 30 minutes.
    Add pineapple.
Mix flour and remaining ingredients to a paste with a
    little water.
Stir into the pickle. Boil for 10 minutes. Bottle.

CELERY PICKLES (with Tamarillos)

- 18 ripe tamarillos
- 5 good heads of celery
- 2 cups brown sugar
- 1½ cups vinegar
- 2 tablespoons salt (or less)
- 1 teaspoon cloves
- 1 teaspoon allspice
- 1 teaspoon cinnamon
- 1 teaspoon mustard

Bring gradually to the boil and simmer for about 1½ hours. Fill warm jars and seal while still warm.

CHOKO PICKLE

- 8 fair-sized chokos, washed
- 450g beans, washed
- salt and water brine
- 1 dessertspoon peppercorns
- 1 level teaspoon cloves
- 1 cup sugar
- 4 cups vinegar
- a little mace
- pinch cayenne
- 450g onions
- 1 teaspoon ginger
- 1 teaspoon curry powder
- 1 dessertspoon flour
- 1 tablespoon mustard
- 1 dessertspoon turmeric

Dice chokos and beans, and stand in weak salt and water for 12 hours. Strain.
Tie spices in a bag. Boil all ingredients in vinegar (except flour, mustard and turmeric) for about 15 minutes.
Add mustard, turmeric and flour blended with a little vinegar. Boil until tender. Bottle when cold.

CUCUMBER PICKLES (Small)

24 small cucumbers, washed and wiped	1 onion
salt	5 whole cloves
water	1 tablespoon mustard seed
vinegar	2 blades mace

Place cucumbers in a jar.
Boil salt and water brine, made strong enough to bear an egg [fresh eggs will float in brine if it contains enough salt].
Cover cucumbers with boiling brine. Leave for 24 hours.
Take out and wipe dry. Place in clean jars.
Cover with hot vinegar spiced with onion, cloves, mustard seed and mace.
Leave for 2 weeks before eating.
If white vinegar is used, they will be a much better colour.

PICKLED CUCUMBERS (Jewish Method)

salt	whole cucumbers, unpeeled
sugar	
grape leaves	

Put a thin layer of salt, sugar then grape leaves in a small barrel or stone jar.
Add cucumbers whole. Repeat until jar is full.
Seal well. Ready in about 2 months.

SWEET PICKLED CUCUMBERS

1.8kg large, full-grown cucumbers, peeled
salt
4 cups boiling vinegar
1 cup sugar
cloves
cinnamon
ginger

Scrape out inside of cucumbers. Cut into pieces. Sprinkle with salt and leave overnight.
Strain the next day. Add boiling vinegar. Let stand 1 day.
Pour off vinegar and boil it with sugar, cloves, cinnamon and ginger (to taste).
When cool, pour over pickle. Put into screw-top jars.
In 2 weeks, pour off vinegar. Reboil and return to pickle when cool. Make airtight.

ECONOMY PICKLE

leftover vinegar from pickled onion bottles
1 cup dates
1 cup raisins
1 cup figs

Boil vinegar with fruit for about 20 minutes.
Press through a sieve. Put in jars and seal.

PICKLED FIGS (Fresh)

cloves
2.7kg figs, unpeeled
4 cups vinegar
1.4kg sugar
1 tablespoon mixed spices (allspice, mace, cinnamon, etc)

Stick 2 or 3 cloves into each fig. Boil vinegar, sugar and spices together. Add figs.
Boil slowly until figs can be pierced with a straw.
Put fruit into hot jars.
Boil syrup for 5 minutes. Pour over figs, and seal while hot.

PICKLED GHERKINS

gherkins
salt and water brine
spiced vinegar – allspice, mace, cloves, etc
(see page 53)

Easy way: place gherkins in brine and leave until yellow.
Drain and put into jars. Cover with hot spiced vinegar.
Put in a warm place until gherkins are green again.
　　Pour off vinegar.
Add a fresh supply of spiced vinegar, and seal jars.

MIXED PICKLE

1.4kg green tomatoes, sliced
2.7kg small onions, peeled
2 or 3 cucumbers with ends removed, cut into small pieces
3 small cauliflowers, separated into small florets
1 small cabbage, shredded
salt and water brine to cover
8 cups vinegar
220g sugar
spices to taste

Put all vegetables in a large basin. Cover with brine and leave overnight.
Drain and rinse well with cold water. Dry.
Pack in jars or bottles. Cover with vinegar boiled with spices and sugar. Cover and store.
This is ready in several weeks.
A little golden syrup may be boiled with the vinegar and spices.

MOTHER'S PICKLE

1 cabbage, cut up very fine
1 white cauliflower
1 large cucumber
900g tomatoes
450g onions
1 small marrow
675 to 900g scarlet runner beans
sprinkling of salt
1 cup water
vinegar to cover vegetables
1 small tin golden syrup
½ cup vinegar

mixed spice to taste	1 level teaspoon mustard
ground cloves to taste	2 tablespoons turmeric
nutmeg to taste	for colouring
cinnamon to taste	flour
curry powder to taste	

Cut all vegetables up fine. Leave in a china bowl overnight with a sprinkling of salt.

Next day, sprinkle with water. Strain off brine.

Put vegetables in a pan and cover with cold vinegar. Bring to the boil.

In a separate saucepan, heat golden syrup with ½ cup vinegar. Pour into hot vegetables.

When cooked, thicken with the spices and enough flour mixed with water to make a paste.

Put in boiling mixture. Cook not more than 6 minutes. Bottle when cool.

Cover with brown paper and make airtight.

MUSHROOMS — Pickled

mushrooms	pepper
salt	spice
vinegar	

Cook mushrooms in their own juice with sprinkling of salt for 30 minutes.

When nearly all liquid has boiled away, cover with vinegar.

Add pepper and spice to taste. Boil for a few minutes.
    Pot and seal.

SWEET MUSTARD PICKLE

about 4kg cut up mixed vegetables (tomatoes, cucumber, onion, cauliflower)
salt
8 cups vinegar
220g treacle or golden syrup
900g sugar
30g mustard
15g ground ginger
¼ teaspoon cayenne pepper
cornflour to thicken
curry powder to thicken

Put vegetables in an earthenware jar, add a handful of salt to each layer and leave overnight.
Next day, drain off liquid, and wash vegetables in water. Put all other ingredients in a pan.
Boil and add vegetables. Boil for 5 minutes, or longer.
Thicken with cornflour and curry powder. Cover while hot.

NASTURTIUM SEEDS

Spread nasturtium seeds in sun for 2 or 3 days to dry.
Put in jars, and sprinkle with salt.
Fill jars with boiled, spiced vinegar (see page 53), and seal when cold.
Leave 2 months before using.
Put green seeds in salt and water for 2 days; then in cold fresh water for 1 day.
Pack into jars, cover with boiling vinegar seasoned with mace, peppercorns and sugar. Cork.

PICKLED ONIONS

4.5kg onions, peeled	900g golden syrup
1 cup salt	30g peppercorns
6 cups vinegar	30g cloves
900g light brown sugar	a few small chillies

Peel onions and keep dry. Sprinkle onions with salt and leave overnight.
Next day, wipe onions. Boil vinegar and other ingredients.
When cold, pour over onions.

Variations
1. Peel onions and place in jars. Add 1 teaspoon sugar and 3 peppercorns (or spices) to each jar. Fill jar with cold vinegar. Cork. Ready in 2 weeks.
2. Peel and wipe 2.7kg onions. Add 8 cups vinegar to a saucepan with a piece of salt the size of an egg (or less), and 450g white sugar. Bring to the boil. While boiling, add onions. Stir carefully for 5 minutes. No spices; onions stay nice and light.

PICKLED ONIONS WITH HONEY

4 cups vinegar
1 cup honey
onions

Mix vinegar and honey well. Put onions in jars, pour over liquid. This is ready in about 4 days.

PICKLED PEACHES

2 cups vinegar
1 teaspoon cinnamon
1½ cups sugar
peaches, stoned
and halved
a few cloves

Put vinegar, cinnamon and sugar in a pot and boil for 10 minutes.
Add peaches. Boil until tender. Lift peaches into hot jars.
Boil syrup again and pour over peaches. Add cloves to each jar and seal tight.
White vinegar may be used.

Sweet Pickled Cucumbers, page 44

Pickled Onions, page 49

PEARS (Pickled with Onion)

900g onions, cut up	¼ teaspoon cayenne pepper
salt	
2.7kg pears	1½ tablespoons curry powder
3 bottles vinegar (9 cups)	
680g sugar	1½ tablespoons mustard
	2 tablespoons flour

Sprinkle onions with salt and leave overnight.
Strain off brine. Cut up pears. Put in a pan with vinegar, onions and sugar.
Boil until tender. Add other ingredients, wet with a little vinegar, and boil a few more minutes.
Bottle and tie down.

PRUNE PICKLE

900g prunes, washed	110g sugar
3 cups vinegar	30g chillies

Prick prunes with a fork. Leave overnight soaking in water.
Strain off water next morning. Put prunes in jars.
Boil vinegar, sugar and chillies. Allow to cool. Pour over prunes.
Stand 1 week before using.

PICKLED SHALLOTS (1)

shallots, peeled
4 cups boiling water
1 small cup salt
4 cups vinegar
¼ cup pickling spices
2 cups honey (or 3 cups sugar)

Add shallots to boiling water and salt, cool. Leave overnight.
Dry shallots with clean muslin and put into jars.
Boil vinegar with pickling spices and honey for 5 to 10 minutes.
Pour over shallots in jars.

PICKLED SHALLOTS (2)

shallots, peeled
a little salt
a few cloves
allspice
4 teaspoons sugar

Put shallots in a big basin and sprinkle with salt. Leave overnight.
Remove shallots, lay on a cloth and remove any skin.
Quarter fill a jar, adding some cloves and some allspice. Repeat until jar is full.
Pour on cold vinegar. Add sugar to top and leave.

GREEN TOMATO PICKLE

2.7kg green tomatoes
2 tablespoons salt
4 cups vinegar
1.4kg onions, peeled and cut up
1 teaspoon allspice
1 teaspoon cayenne pepper
2 tablespoons curry powder
1 cup golden syrup
flour to thicken

Cut up tomatoes and sprinkle with salt. Stand for 6 hours.
Strain and cover with vinegar. Bring to the boil.
Add onions, spices and golden syrup.
Simmer 1 hour and thicken with flour. Bottle hot.

VINEGAR (Spiced)

4 cups vinegar
10g cinnamon
10g whole cloves
10g mace
10g root ginger
3 or 4 peppercorns
pinch of cayenne pepper

Heat vinegar in a pan, covered. When it cools, add spices in a muslin bag.
Cool, and remove spice bag.
Note: Cold vinegar is best for crisp pickles such as onions and cabbage. Hot vinegar should be used for softer pickles, such as walnuts, plums, beetroot or mushrooms.

WALNUTS (Sweet Pickled)

Gather walnuts in early December — prick well with a fork.

walnuts	piece of stick cinnamon (or
water	½ teaspoon powdered
4 cups boiling water	cinnamon)
1 tablespoon cloves	2 cups vinegar
1 tablespoon allspice	450g sugar

Put walnuts into jar and cover with water. Change water every day for a week.

Strain and put in boiling water with spices. Boil until tender.

Pour off water and spices. Boil vinegar and sugar and add to walnuts.

Stand for 1 week. Strain off vinegar and bring to the boil.

Put walnuts in bottles, pour over boiling vinegar, and screw down.

Mint Sauce (Preserved), page 58

Mushroom Ketchup (2), page 59

PICKLED GREEN WALNUTS
Pick walnuts early in the season.

about 100 walnuts, pricked all over
4 cups water
170g salt
8 cups vinegar

60g black pepper
80g ginger
80g cloves
60g mustard seed

Place walnuts in brine of the salt and water.
Change brine every 3 days and keep stirring about. This takes about 9 days until they go black.
Boil up vinegar and remaining ingredients for about 10 minutes.
Strain and pour over walnuts in glass bottles.

Sauces & Ketchups

MINT SAUCE (Preserved)

225g sugar
½ cup vinegar
½ cup water

1 teacup finely chopped mint
salt and pepper to taste

Put sugar, vinegar and water in pan and bring to the boil. Boil for 5 minutes. Cool.
Add mint and seasoning. Pour into small bottles and use as required.
You may need a little extra hot water when using sauce.

MUSHROOM KETCHUP (1)

freshly picked mushrooms
salt
black peppercorns

a little cayenne pepper
cloves
a little mace

Put mushrooms in an earthenware basin and sprinkle with salt. Leave overnight or longer.
Bring slowly to the boil, and simmer 30 to 40 minutes. Strain through muslin.
Put liquid on again, add other ingredients, and boil another 30 to 35 minutes.
Strain all. Bottle when cold. Should keep for about 2 years.

MUSHROOM KETCHUP (2)

fresh mushrooms, wiped
salt
4 cups mushroom juice (when cooked)
30g peppercorns
30g allspice
1 blade of mace or a little powdered mace
15g root ginger

Sprinkle mushrooms with salt. Put in a large crock, covered with a damp cloth, and leave in a warm place for 24 hours. Mash well and strain.
To each 4 cups juice, add 30g peppercorns. Boil for 30 minutes. Add allspice, mace and ginger. Simmer another 15 minutes.
Remove from heat and let get cold. Boil again for 15 minutes, and cool again.
Reboil for 15 minutes, then strain, bottle and seal.
This is a very old recipe, and the repeated boiling is a special feature — it makes the best ketchup. Boiling may be repeated as many as 6 times.

PLUM SAUCE

2.7kg dark plums
6 cups vinegar
900g sugar
1 teaspoon cayenne
 pepper
6 teaspoons salt

2 teaspoons ground cloves
2 teaspoons ground ginger
1 teaspoon black or white
 pepper
1 teaspoon ground mace
30g garlic

Boil all together until pulpy.
Strain through a colander.
Bottle when cold. Should keep well.

TAMARILLO SAUCE

3.6kg tamarillos
2 large onions
900g apples
900g brown sugar
110g salt

60g black pepper
30g allspice
15g cayenne pepper
4 cups vinegar
30g cloves

Boil all for 4 hours and strain.

Plum Sauce, page 60

Tomato Sauce, page 61

TOMATO KETCHUP (No Spice)

5 to 6kg ripe tomatoes
6 medium onions
½ cup salt
1 teaspoon cayenne
pepper
3 cups sugar
2½ cups vinegar
3 tablespoons cornflour

Cut up tomatoes and onions. Sprinkle with salt and leave overnight.
Boil until soft and put through a sieve.
Bring to the boil again with cayenne, sugar and vinegar. Boil about 1½ hours.
Thicken with cornflour mixed with a little of the cooled mixture.
Boil another 3 or 4 minutes. Bottle and seal.

TOMATO SAUCE

pinch cayenne pepper
80g whole spice
15g cloves
15g ground ginger
3.6kg sliced tomatoes
3 large onions, sliced
3 large cooking apples, unpeeled, cored and cut up
80g salt
900g light brown sugar
4 cups vinegar

Put all spices in a muslin bag. Boil all ingredients together for 3 hours.
Strain and boil again for 30 minutes. The second boiling is absolutely necessary.
Cork or seal tightly.

TOMATO SAUCE WITHOUT VINEGAR

4.5kg tomatoes
450g apples
3 onions
juice of 5 or 6 lemons
110g salt
340g white sugar
20g whole cloves
30g allspice

Cut tomatoes and apples in pieces without peeling.
Peel onions and cut into cubes. Add other ingredients.
Boil for 2 hours. Rub through a fine sieve.
Boil up again. Put into sterilised bottles. Cork tightly.

BRIGHT RED PURE TOMATO SAUCE

5.4kg ripe tomatoes, washed and cut up
80g allspice
1.4kg brown sugar
3 cups vinegar
80g salt

Put all ingredients (with spices tied up in muslin) in a pan and boil for 3 hours. Stir frequently.
When cooked, put through a colander and bottle. Cork when cold.

GREEN TOMATO SAUCE

3.6kg green tomatoes
900g apples
450g onions
5 cups vinegar
900g sugar
110g salt

¼ teaspoon cayenne pepper
30g each of peppercorns, allspice and cloves, tied in muslin

Cut up and boil tomatoes, apples and onions with half the vinegar and other ingredients for 45 minutes.
Strain. Add remaining vinegar and boil another 45 minutes.
Bottle and cork when cold.

WORCESTERSHIRE SAUCE (Quite Hot)

16 cups vinegar
1.35kg apples (pulpy)
900g brown sugar
6 cloves garlic
2 teaspoons cayenne pepper

2 tablespoons ground ginger
4 tablespoons salt
2 tablespoons cloves
peel of 1 orange, grated fine

Boil for 2 hours. Strain and bottle.
This is a good sauce. It keeps well and can be recommended.

Jams & Jellies

AUNT DAISY'S TIPS FOR SUCCESSFUL JAMS & JELLIES

- When making plum jam always put in plenty of stones as they help the jam to set.
- Boil fruit and water well before adding sugar. Add the sugar warm, stir until dissolved, and then give the jam a good rolling boil.
- When jam sets too thick, add enough boiling water to the pot to make the right consistency. Or empty pot into a saucepan and add boiling water. It sets right when cold.
- When making blackberry jam, put the berries through the mincer, making sure all the juice is caught and saved. Makes nice even jam, with no lumps.
- Sugar must be well dissolved before the jam is brought back to the boil again.
- Making jam from pulp — allow ¾ to 1 cup sugar for each cup of pulp, and add the juice of 1 or 2 lemons.
- Put about ½ teaspoon salt to 2.7kg (say) of jam about 15 minutes before taking up. Helps to settle scum, and clears the jam.
- When mildew forms on top — scrape off mildew, brush top of jam with vinegar, then fit in rounds of paper

brushed in vinegar, and screw down. Vinegar discourages growth of mould.
- Jam gone sugary — stand jar in warm oven, until melted. Then stir in a little boiling water, to make sure that sugar is thoroughly dissolved.
- A packet of jelly crystals will help set obstinate jam. Or a little gelatine. Or the juice of 1 or 2 lemons added before jam comes off the boil. Or 1 teaspoon citric acid.
- Jelly-jams should cool a little in the pan before being bottled, and then there should be no settling of the thick part in bottom of the jars.
- Japonica apples added to jelly help it set, and give a nice flavour.
- When jam has burnt, try stirring in a little peanut butter. Or reboil with a small teaspoon of baking soda.
- Stir jam with a wooden or silver spoon.
- Jam made from over-ripe fruit will not keep.
- A knob of butter put in just before dishing up jam will help it set, and remove scum.
- Pack jams and pickles at the bottom of the cupboard, as the top is hotter.
- Jam from jelly pulp — after straining fruit for jelly, to each cup of pulp add ¾ cup of sugar and about 3 tablespoons of water. Stir well and boil for 10 minutes.
- If cellophane labels stick together, hold them over the steam from a kettle and they will curl apart.

STANDARD JAM METHOD

An experienced and successful home-maker uses this recipe for all jam making:

> 2.7kg fruit (not too ripe)
> 12 cups water
> 225g sugar

The fruit may all be of one kind, or mixed, say 1.8kg plums, 900g raspberries, etc.
Boil fruit slowly in water until tender, and have the sugar warmed.
Stir in sugar, continue stirring until thoroughly dissolved, and then boil hard, a rolling boil, until it will set when tested; sometimes 45 minutes, sometimes less, or more, according to the fruit.
If desired, jam can be strained to get out seeds or skins.

APPLE JELLY

> 2.7kg unripe apples, cut into small pieces, with skins and cores
> water
> 1 cup sugar to each 1 cup liquid from cooked fruit
> juice of 2 lemons
> 1 teaspoon salt
> 1 tablespoon butter
> 1 bottle raspberry essence (or strawberry, or lime with a little food colouring)

Barely cover apples with water. Boil for about 30 minutes.
Leave until cool. Strain through a jelly bag overnight.
Next day, measure liquid and bring to the boil. Add sugar to liquid, the lemon juice, salt and butter.
Take off heat, and stir in raspberry essence. Stir well and bottle hot.

APRICOT GINGER

This is a lovely refreshing jam that can be made any time of the year, as apricot pulp is used.

grated rind of 3 or 4 lemons	3kg sugar
1 cup water	juice of 3 or 4 lemons
3.4kg tinned apricot pulp	220g finely chopped preserved ginger

Cook lemon rinds in the water for about 1 hour.
Put apricot pulp, sugar, lemon juice, cooked rind and preserved ginger in a preserving pan.
Bring to the boil and keep boiling until thick, about 15 minutes.

APRICOT & LEMON JAM

450g dried apricots	2.25kg sugar
10 cups boiling water	450g lemons

Pour boiling water over the apricots, and soak overnight.
Boil lemons until tender. Drain well.
When cold slice very thinly, removing the pips.
Boil apricots until pulpy, add lemons and sugar and boil until jam sets, about 1 hour.

APRICOT & ORANGE JAM

900g washed and dried apricots
grated rind of 5 oranges
pulp of 5 oranges, sliced
14 breakfast cups water
3.6kg sugar

Soak apricots with grated rind and sliced orange pulp in water for 24 hours.
Next day, bring to the boil, and boil for 30 minutes.
Add sugar, and boil another 30 minutes, stirring constantly, until it jellies.

APRICOT & PINEAPPLE JAM

900g dried apricot
10 cups hot water
a little baking soda
3kg sugar, warmed
2 tins crushed pineapple

Wash apricots in hot water and a little baking soda. Soak all night with the water.
Next day, boil for 30 to 40 minutes.
Add sugar and pineapple. Boil until it will set, about 30 to 45 minutes, stirring constantly.
Half quantities may be used.

Apricot & Pineapple Jam, page 70

Cranberry Jelly, page 76

APRICOT JAM (Fresh)

450g apricots, weighed once
   cut in half and stones removed
450g sugar

Wipe fruit with a damp cloth. Lay in a pan, with layers of sugar, and stand overnight.
Next day, bring slowly to the boil, stirring constantly for 30 to 45 minutes, until it will set.
Can be made in larger quantities.

BLACKBERRY JAM

450g blackberries
½ cup water
570g sugar

Boil fruit and water together for 30 minutes.
Break up berries with a potato masher.
Add sugar and boil until it jellies, 20 to 30 minutes.
This makes excellent jam. Can be made in larger quantities.

BLACKBERRY & APPLE JELLY

900g apples
2.7kg blackberries
water

1 cup sugar to each cup juice

Chop apples, including skins and cores.
Place in a preserving pan with blackberries and water to cover.
Cook until soft. Strain through a jelly bag.
Measure juice and bring to the boil. Stir in sugar gradually.
When sugar is dissolved, boil fast until a little jellies when tested on a saucer, about 30 to 45 minutes.

BLACKBERRY & CRAB APPLE JELLY

Roughly equal quantities of fruit.

crab apples, halved and quartered
blackberries, crushed

water
450g preheated sugar to each 2 cups liquid

Put fruit in a pan with water and simmer for 1 hour with lid off.
Strain through a flannel for not more than 24 hours.
Measure the liquid and bring to the boil.
Add sugar gradually, stirring all the time to completely dissolve sugar.
Bring quickly back to boil and boil fast until it will set, probably about 5 to 10 minutes.

BLACKBERRY & ELDERBERRY JAM

Equal quantities of fruit.

　　blackberries, stalks removed
　　elderberries, stalks removed
　　340g sugar for every 450g fruit

Put fruit in a preserving pan. Squeeze slightly and bring to the boil. Boil for 20 minutes.

Put sugar in a dish and warm in the oven before adding to the fruit.

Add sugar and bring to the boil again.

Boil again for 20 minutes or until jam will set when tested on a plate.

BLACKBERRY & PLUM JAM

　　900g plums
　　2 cups water
　　2.25kg blackberries
　　2.5kg sugar, warmed
　　tartaric acid or citric acid

Stew plums and water. Add blackberries and boil until soft, about 15 minutes. Stir.

Add sugar and stir until dissolved.

Ten minutes before taking up add 1 small teaspoon tartaric acid or citric acid.

Jams & Jellies

BLACK CURRANT JAM (1)

For every 450g black currants,
allow 1½ breakfast cups juice from stewed
rhubarb and 680g sugar

Boil black currants and rhubarb juice together for 10 minutes.
Add sugar and stir until dissolved.
Boil for about 5 minutes. Test before bottling.

BLACK CURRANT JAM (2)

1.4kg black currants
3 cups water
2kg sugar
juice of 1 lemon

Boil fruit in water for 10 minutes.
Add sugar and lemon juice, and boil fast for 45 minutes.
Test before bottling.

CAPE GOOSEBERRY JAM

2.25kg cape gooseberries
2.25kg sugar
4 cups water

Boil sugar and water for 10 minutes.
Add berries and boil hard until jam sets when tested.
Bottle when cool.

CAPE GOOSEBERRY & LEMON JAM

2.25kg sugar
2 cups water
juice of 5 lemons

2.25kg cape gooseberries, shelled

Boil sugar and water in a pan. Add lemon juice.
When syrup is quite clear add gooseberries. They may be pricked with a needle.
Boil for about 1½ hours, or until will set when tested.

CHERRY & RED CURRANT JAM

1.8kg cherries
2 cups red currant juice (fruit boiled in a little water until mushy, then strained)

2 cups sugar to every 2 cups cherries when cooked

Simmer cherries until soft. Add equal measured quantity of sugar.
Stir until sugar is dissolved.
Boil until jam will set when tested.
Bottle when it has cooked a little.

CHOKO & PASSIONFRUIT JAM

3.6kg chokos, peeled and sliced
3.2kg sugar
1 cup boiling water
juice of 6 lemons
36 passionfruit

Cut up chokos. Add 6 cups of the sugar and stand for 24 hours.
Next day, add boiling water and boil until clear.
Add lemon juice and remaining sugar. Stir until dissolved.
Cool rapidly until it will set. Add passionfruit.
Boil about 3 minutes. Seal cold.

CRANBERRY JELLY

1.8kg cranberries
4 cups water
1½ to 2 cups sugar for each 2 cups juice

Put cranberries in a pan with water. When tender, strain off juice.
Measure and put back in the pan. Add sugar.
Stir and skim until sugar has dissolved.
Simmer, not hard boil, and take up as soon as it will set.

DAMSON JAM (without Stones)

3.6kg damsons
water
2.7kg sugar

Boil damsons with very little water until tender.
Strain through a sieve. Add sugar and stir until dissolved.
Boil until it will set when tested.

ELDERBERRY JELLY
Gather berries while dry.

elderberries	water
1/3 quantity of apples (or jelly apples) to 1 quantity elderberries	1 cup sugar to 1 cup liquid from berries and apple

Pick off elderberry stems and clean. Leave smaller stems on.
Cut up apples as for apple jelly and add.
Barely cover with water and leave overnight.
Next day, boil up until soft and pulpy. Strain through muslin.
    Leave again overnight.
Next day, add sugar, and stir until dissolved. Boil up until set.

ELDERBERRY & APPLE JAM

    1.8kg cooking apples, cored and cut up
    1.4kg elderberries, stalks removed

    340g (1½ cups) sugar to each 900g fruit

Boil together apples and elderberries until soft. Add sugar. Stir until dissolved and boil until it will set, about 30 minutes.

FEIJOA JAM

Do not peel feijoas.

    2.25kg feijoas, cut into thin slices

    8 cups water
    2.7kg sugar

Put feijoas and water in a pan. Cook until soft.
Add sugar gradually, stirring all the time.
Bring carefully to the boil, still stirring; keep at a fast rolling boil until jam sets when tested.
Feijoa jam must be watched, as it jellies quickly.

FEIJOA, GUAVA & APPLE JELLY

1.4kg feijoas
450g ordinary red guavas
900g small apples

1 cup sugar to each
1 cup juice

Cut up fruit roughly and boil until well pulped (about 1 hour).
Strain well. Boil the juice with sugar until a little jells, about
10 minutes.

FIG CONSERVE (Fresh)

3.6kg peeled figs
2.7kg sugar

450g preserved ginger
juice of 4 or 5 lemons

Cut figs in halves or quarters. Put in a pan with sugar and
ginger.
Pour over lemon juice. Heat slowly until sugar is dissolved,
stirring gently.
Boil fast for 1½ hours, or until sets when tested.

FIG JAM (Fresh)

1.2kg figs, tailed and cut up small
220g apples, peeled and cut up small
¼ cup preserved ginger, cut small
1.4kg sugar
½ breakfast cup lemon juice
2½ breakfast cups water

Add all ingredients to a preserving pan. Bring slowly to the boil. Boil about 40 minutes. Test before taking up.
A lovely amber colour.

FIVE-MINUTE BERRY JAM

Suitable for strawberries, loganberries, raspberries, gooseberries, or red or black currants.

2.7kg fruit
2.7kg sugar
pinch of salt

Put fruit in a pan. Sprinkle over 2 cups of the sugar. Boil for exactly 5 minutes.
Add remaining sugar, and stir until dissolved. Bring to the boil again.
Boil fast for exactly 5 minutes (work by the clock).
When cold, should be a beautiful firm jam.

Feijoa Jam, page 78

Five-Minute Berry Jam, page 80

FRUIT SALAD JAM (Fresh) (1)

900g peaches
900g apricots
10 bananas
1 tin crushed pineapple
1 lemon, no skin or pips

pulp of 4 or more passionfruit
2 oranges, no skin or pips
2.25kg sugar

Cut up peaches, apricots and bananas.
Add pineapple, lemon and orange pulp, passionfruit pulp and sugar.
Boil for about 20 minutes, until fruit is cooked and jam will set when tested.

FRUIT SALAD JAM (Fresh) (2)

900g apples
900g plums
900g pears
900g apricots

4 cups water
3.6kg sugar
2 oranges
2 lemons

Peel and stone fruit. Put peel and stones in the water and boil for 30 minutes.
Strain, and put liquid back into the pan with sugar.
Bring to the boil, stirring all the time. Add juice and a little pulp of oranges and lemons.
Add cut-up fruit. Boil about 45 minutes, or until it will set.

GOOSEBERRY JAM

450g gooseberries
2 cups water
900g sugar

Boil fruit and water together for 20 minutes.
Add sugar, dissolve, and boil fast for about 40 minutes, or until it will set when tested.
Three times this amount of gooseberries makes a lot of jam by this recipe. May be made in larger quantities.

GOOSEBERRY MINT JELLY

green gooseberries, washed
cold water
2 cups sugar
stalks of fresh mint, tied in a bundle

Put gooseberries in a pan and nearly cover with water. Cook until pulpy.
Strain through a sieve and add sugar. Add mint and boil until setting stage.
Remove mint. Bottle jelly.
Eat with cold meat.

GRAPE JELLY

freshly picked grapes
2 cups sugar to each 2 cups juice

Put grapes, stalks and all, into a pan. Nearly cover with water. Boil until mashed. Strain through a jelly bag.
Bring juice to the boil, and boil for a few minutes.
Add sugar, and boil until it will set.

GREEN GOOSEBERRY & CHERRY PLUM JAM

1.4kg green gooseberries
1.4kg cherry plums
12 cups water
2.5 to 3.5kg sugar, warmed

Boil fruit and water for 30 minutes, or until soft.
Add sugar and dissolve, stirring.
Boil quickly until will set when tested.

GREEN GOOSEBERRY MARMALADE

2 lemons
2 small breakfast cups boiling water
1.4kg green gooseberries
3 small breakfast cups cold water
2.7kg sugar, warmed

Shred lemons as for marmalade. Cover with the boiling water and leave overnight.
Next day, boil up with gooseberries and the cold water, for 1 hour.
Add sugar and stir until dissolved. Bring to the boil and hard boil for not more than 10 minutes.
Delicious. Green in colour. Test for setting.

GREEN GRAPE JAM

900g grapes
1 teacup water
790g sugar
¼ teaspoon citric acid

Put grapes and water in a pan. Press and cook until soft.
Add sugar and boil until it will set.
Strain through a strainer to get out skins and seeds.
Add citric acid. Essence may be added if liked.

GUAVA JELLY

    8 cups guavas   water
    2 lemons   sugar, warmed

Cut guavas and lemons. Put in a preserving pan and cover with water.
Simmer about 2 hours then strain through a jelly bag.
Measure the liquid obtained. Add 1 cup sugar to each 1 cup juice.
Bring juice to the boil, and stir until dissolved. Boil hard until it will set.
Pour into heated jelly jars and allow to cool.
Pour melted wax over then cover the jars. Store in a cool, dark cupboard.
A beautiful red jelly which can be served in the usual way or as a condiment with cold lamb or veal.

HAWTHORN JELLY

    hawthorn berries   juice of 1 lemon to each
    cold water   2 cups liquid
    1 cup sugar to each 1 cup liquid

Wash and put hawthorn berries into a big preserving pan. Add enough water to three-parts cover them.
Cover and simmer gently for 1½ hours. Leave overnight.
Next day, bring to the boil then strain through a jelly bag.
Measure the liquid, bring to the boil and add sugar. Add lemon juice.
Boil briskly for 1 hour or until it will set when tested. Bottle hot, seal cold.

JAPONICA & APPLE JELLY

900g japonica apples
900g cooking apples
1 cup sugar to each 1 cup fruit pulp

Cut up fruit. Cover with water and boil until soft.
Leave until cold. Strain through a jelly bag.
Next day, measure juice and bring to the boil.
Gradually add sugar and boil until it sets when tested, about 20 minutes.

JAPONICA JELLY

japonica apples
cold water
1 cup sugar to each 1 cup juice
juice of 1 lemon to each 1.35kg japonicas

Cut up apples, put in a pan. Add cold water, but not enough to cover.
Cover and cook until tender. Strain overnight.
Next day, measure juice and bring to the boil. Add sugar and boil until it will set.
Sets quickly. Lemon juice improves the flavour of this jelly.

LAUREL BERRY & APPLE JAM

1.4kg laurel berries
1.2kg cut-up apples
water

1 heaped cup sugar to each 1 cup juice

Cover fruit scantily with water in a pan.
Boil to a pulp and strain through muslin bag. Leave overnight.
Bring to the boil. Add sugar.
Boil quickly for 30 minutes or until jam will set.

KIWIFRUIT JAM

kiwifruit
1½ cups sugar to every 2 cups pulp

Cut kiwifruit in half and scoop out pulp. Cover the bottom of a pan with water.
Add fruit pulp and boil until cooked. Add sugar to measured fruit pulp.
Stir until dissolved. Boil again until it will set when tested.
Vary by cooking in lemon juice and water.

KIWIFRUIT & ORANGE JAM

2kg kiwifruit pulp
2.25kg sugar

juice and grated rind
of 2 lemons

Boil all together until it sets.

LOGANBERRY JAM

Do not have fruit too ripe.

450g loganberries
1 cup water
570g sugar, warmed

Boil fruit and water.
Add sugar, dissolve, and boil until it will set, about 15 minutes.
Can make in larger quantities.

LOGANBERRY & PLUM JAM

2.7kg plums
900g loganberries
12 cups sugar, warmed

Boil plums with a little water. Add loganberries and cook until soft. Add sugar and boil until it will set.

MARMALADE (Dundee)

1.4kg sweet oranges
2 lemons
12 large cups water
4kg sugar, warmed

Slice or mince the fruit. Leave to soak in water for 24 hours.
Boil for 20 minutes. Leave 34 hours again.
Boil again, add sugar and boil again until will set when tested, about 20 minutes.
Bottle while hot.

MARMALADE (Easy)

oranges, lemons or grapefruit
2 cups water for every
piece of fruit
450g sugar for every piece of fruit

Cut up fruit, cover with correct amount of water. Leave 12 hours.
Next day, boil slowly until soft. Add sugar and boil quickly until it sets.

MARMALADE — NZ Grapefruit (Johnny's)

450g grapefruit
6 cups water

1 cup sugar to each cup of pulp

Cut fruit very finely. Weigh. Add water. Let stand for 36 hours.
Bring quietly to the boil and boil 1½ hours. Take off and leave overnight.
Weigh again and add sugar. Boil until it will set when tested.
Can be made in larger quantities.

MARMALADE (Prize)

6 New Zealand grapefruit (or 4 grapefruit and 2 sweet oranges)

12 breakfast cups water
4kg sugar

Cut up fruit very finely. Add water and leave for 12 hours.
Bring to the boil and boil until soft. Leave overnight.
Boil for 30 minutes. Add sugar, and boil for 45 minutes to 1 hour, or until it will set.
Makes good jelly — not too sweet and not too bitter.

Marmalade (Prize), page 90

Parsley Jelly, page 97

MARMALADE WITH GREEN TOMATOES

2.7kg green tomatoes
6 lemons, minced, skins and all
2.7kg sugar
water

Slice tomatoes, add lemon juice and very little water.
Cook until tender and soft.
Stir in sugar and boil fast until it will set when tested.

MARROW JAM

1.4kg vegetable marrow, peeled and pips removed
juice of 2 lemons
rind of 2 lemons cut finely
1.4kg sugar
30g ground ginger
ginger tied in a muslin bag

Cut marrow into pieces about 5cm long. Put into a pan.
Add lemon juice and rind. Add sugar and ginger.
Boil until clear and soft, about 1 hour. Seal cold.

MARROW & QUINCE JAM

2.7kg marrow, peeled and minced
2.7kg sugar
1.8kg quinces, minced
2kg sugar

Cover marrow with 12 cups sugar and leave overnight.
Next day, add quinces and the remainder of sugar. Boil together for about 3 hours until set.

MEDLAR JAM

1.4kg medlars, washed
1 cup water
juice of 2 lemons
1.4kg sugar

Put medlars into a preserving pan with water and lemon juice.
Stand over a slow heat, and simmer for 1 hour.
Strain with a dish underneath.
Mash with a wooden spoon, taking care no pips pass through.
Put back into pan and add sugar. Boil fast for about 45 minutes.
Put in jars and cover as usual.

MELON JAM

　　1 small melon
　　2 cups sugar for each cup of fruit
　　1 cup water to each 1 cup melon
　　juice and rind of 1 lemon for every
　　　　450g melon (or ½ an orange, or 1 medium pineapple, cut up)

Cut up melon small. Sprinkle half the sugar right through melon and leave overnight.
Next day, add water and simmer gently until soft — may be 2 hours.
Add remaining sugar, stir until dissolved. Then boil rapidly.
Flavour with lemon juice and rind.

MELON JAM (Never Fails)
Do not let the cut fruit stand.

5.4kg melons	4kg sugar
juice and grated rind of 6 oranges	220g finely cut preserved ginger
4 cups water	

Cut melon into cubes. Add orange juice and rind, and water, and boil.
Stir carefully for 30 minutes until tender. Add sugar and ginger.
Boil until golden brown.

MELON & PASSIONFRUIT JAM

2.7kg pie melon, cut up
450g sugar

pulp of 48 passionfruit, tied in muslin
450g sugar

Put melon in a basin with sugar. Leave overnight. Put melon, passionfruit and sugar in a preserving pan. Boil for 2½ to 3 hours. Excellent.

MELON & TAMARILLO JAM

1.4kg yellow tamarillos
boiling water
4.5kg pie melon, cut up

juice and rind of 3 lemons (if liked)
450g sugar to each 450g fruit

Pour boiling water over tamarillos. Skin and cut up. Add melon. Put all in a pan, bring to the boil, and add about half the sugar. Boil again, adding remaining sugar. Boil until will set when tested.

MINT & APPLE JELLY

900g windfall apples, quartered (unpeeled)
water

4 tablespoons chopped green mint
½ cup sugar to each 1 cup of juice

Almost cover apples with water. Boil for 10 minutes.
Add mint. Boil 20 minutes, then strain.
Add sugar and boil until it will set when tested.

MOCK RASPBERRY JAM (or Strawberry)
The recipe is extremely popular and very delicious.

1.8kg tomatoes
1.4kg sugar
juice of 1 lemon

1 tablespoon raspberry or strawberry essence

Skin tomatoes and cut up fairly fine. Add sugar and lemon juice.
Boil gently for about 2 hours. Stir in essence.
Do not boil after essence is added, or flavour is lost.
    Test for setting.

MULBERRY JAM

2.7kg mulberries
2.25kg sugar
1 small teaspoon citric acid

Boil fruit without sugar for 15 minutes.
Crush a few to start juice flowing, or add 1 tablespoon water.
Heat sugar for browning. Pour in sugar, which should be hot enough to keep jam boiling.
Boil quickly for 45 minutes. Add citric acid a few minutes before taking off heat.

NECTARINE JAM

2.7kg stoned nectarines, washed but not peeled
2 cups water
juice of 2 lemons
1 dessertspoon butter
kernels of about ¼ of the fruit
2kg sugar, warmed

Cut nectarines into pieces. Put into a pan with the water, butter, lemon juice and kernels.
Boil until soft. Add sugar, about 2 cups at a time.
Boil, stirring well, for about 1 hour. Test before taking up.

PARSLEY JELLY

450g fresh parsley
water
juice of 1 or 2 lemons

1 cup sugar to each 1 cup liquid from parsley

Press parsley down and barely cover with water. Simmer 1 hour.
Add lemon juice and simmer for 10 minutes. Strain through muslin.
Bring to the boil, add sugar, and simmer until it jells.

PASSIONFRUIT JAM

passionfruit
¾ cup of warmed sugar to each 1 cup pulp

Wash passionfruit well, cut in halves, scoop out the pulp.
Put skins on to boil for about 30 minutes or until tender.
Scoop out the soft part, leaving skins like thin paper. Discard skins.
Add pulp to the seed pulp. Add sugar.
Boil until it will set, about 1½ hours. Or may be added to melon jam.

PASSIONFRUIT & APPLE JAM

    passionfruit
    1 cup grated apple to each
      2 cups fruit
    340g sugar to each 450g
    mixed fruit

Cut passionfruit and scoop out insides. Boil skins until tender. Remove pulp inside the skins. Add to the seeds with apple. Boil. When fruit is cooked add sugar. Boil until it will set, as usual.

PASSIONFRUIT & TOMATO JAM

    15 to 20 passionfruit
    2.7kg tomatoes, skins removed by putting into hot water
    2kg sugar

Scoop seeds from passionfruit. Boil skins in water until soft. Add pulp to the seeds. Cut up tomatoes and boil with sugar until melted.
Add passionfruit pulp. Boil for 20 minutes, or until it will set.

PEACH JAM (1)

2.7kg peaches   2kg sugar
butter   1 to 2 cups water

Slice peaches, remove stones, and put in a well-buttered preserving pan with water.
Bring to the boil and cook 5 minutes.
Add sugar. Boil swiftly until a little will set when tested.

PEACH JAM (2) (Good)

1.4kg peaches   1 tablespoon butter
6 cups water   juice of 1 lemon
2.25kg sugar

Cut up peaches and boil in water until soft. Add sugar, butter and lemon juice.
Boil very hard, stirring frequently, until a lovely golden colour and will set — about 45 minutes. Not too stiff.
These proportions may be used for plums, apricots and nectarines.

PEACH JAM (3)

peaches	water
340g sugar to each 450g stoned fruit	a few pieces root ginger (if desired)

Peel peaches and cut into thin slices. Cover with some of the sugar and leave overnight.
Next day, boil with a little water for 30 minutes or until tender.
Add remaining sugar, heated in the oven so that boiling continues.
This is improved by adding ginger. Take ginger out before bottling.

DRIED PEACH JAM

450g dried peaches, cut up	8 cups water
2 lemons, sliced finely	2.25kg sugar

Soak peaches and lemons overnight in water.
Next day, boil up. Add sugar and boil until it sets, about 20 minutes.

Plum Jam, page 103

Three Fruit Jelly, page 115

PEACH & PASSIONFRUIT JAM

2.7kg peaches (not too ripe), peeled and stoned
2.7kg sugar
24 or more passionfruit
juice of 2 lemons
1 extra cup sugar

Cut peaches into pieces. Sprinkle with a little of the sugar. Leave a while.
Scoop out pulp of passionfruit. Boil skins until soft. Scoop out pulp from inside skins and add to seed mixture.
Boil peaches until soft. Add remaining sugar and boil for 1 hour.
Add passionfruit mixture, lemon juice and extra sugar.
Boil until it will set when tested.

PEAR & PASSIONFRUIT JAM

1.4kg sugar
2 cups water
1.8kg pears, peeled and cut up
1½ cups passionfruit pulp

Boil sugar and water for 5 minutes. Drop in pears and simmer for about 1 hour.
Add passionfruit pulp and simmer until a good colour and consistency.
If preferred without the passionfruit seed, the pulp should be whisked well with an egg beater, then strained.

PEAR GINGER (with Lemon Juice)

2.7kg pears
2kg sugar
2 lemons, minced
1 cup finely cut preserved ginger

Peel and cut pears into eighths. Sprinkle with half the sugar. Leave 24 hours covered over.
Add remaining sugar, lemons and ginger.
Boil about 2 hours and test before taking up.

PERSIMMON JELLY
Use ripe fruit.

persimmons, skinned
water
juice of 1 strained lemon to each 2 cups juice
2 cups warmed sugar to each 2 cups juice

Put fruit in a pan. Cover lightly with water. Boil briskly for 2 hours.
Strain through muslin. Measure juice and add lemon juice. Boil.
Add sugar and stir until sugar is dissolved.
Boil rapidly until jelly will set when tested.

PINEAPPLE & PEACH JAM

1 large ripe pineapple
3.2kg peaches
juice of 3 lemons

115g warmed sugar to each 450g prepared fruit

Peel and mince pineapple, removing hard core. Peel and stone peaches.
Put into a preserving pan with lemon juice and bring slowly to the boil.
Cook gently for 30 minutes. Add sugar and boil until it will set when tested.

PLUM JAM (Good)

1.4kg plums
3 breakfast cups water
5 breakfast cups sugar

Put fruit and water in a pan and cook until plums are soft.
Add sugar and boil swiftly until a little tried will set firmly.
Remove stones as they rise to the surface.
Let cool a little before bottling.

PLUM & BLACK CURRANT JAM

1.8kg plums, peeled, halved and stoned
1.4kg black currants
4 cups water
3.2kg sugar

Boil fruit in water until soft. Rub through a colander.
Put into a pan, and bring to the boil.
Slowly add sugar and boil for 40 minutes, or until it will set when tested.
Raspberries can be done the same way.

PLUM & RASPBERRY JAM

1.4kg red plums
water
3.2kg raspberries
4.5kg sugar
pinch of salt

Cover plums with water. Boil for 1 hour then strain through a colander.
Put raspberries in a preserving pan. Add plum pulp and cook for a few minutes.
Add sugar slowly. Add salt.
Bring to the boil and boil quickly for 30 minutes or until it will set.

PRUNE & RHUBARB JAM

3.6kg rhubarb
4.5kg sugar
1.8kg prunes
6 lemons, cut in quarters

Cut rhubarb small and cover with 4 cups of the sugar. Leave overnight.
Wash prunes and soak overnight in enough water to cover.
Next day, put rhubarb in a preserving pan with prunes, water and lemons.
Add remaining sugar. Boil fast for 30 minutes, or until it will set when tested.
Remove the lemons. Pour jam into hot jars, and seal.

PUMPKIN JAM

2.25kg pumpkin, cut into 1cm cubes
2kg sugar
2 oranges
1 lemon
1 teaspoon ground ginger
pinch of cayenne pepper
½ teaspoon citric acid

Cover pumpkin with some of the sugar and leave overnight.
Put oranges and lemon through mincer, catching the juice.
Add fruit, juice and ginger to pumpkin. Boil slowly until clear.
Add remaining sugar and stir until dissolved. Bring to the boil.
Add cayenne and citric acid and boil until it will set.

QUINCE CONSERVE

3.2kg quinces
14 cups water
4kg sugar

Wipe quinces well, put in a pan with water and boil until soft.
Take out, peel and core, and cut into suitable pieces.
Add half the sugar to the water. Add quinces and boil for
　　30 minutes.
Add remaining sugar. Cook until a bright colour and will set
　　when tested, about 45 minutes after last sugar is added.

QUINCE HONEY

6 large quinces, peeled, cored and minced (peel and core retained)
hot water
8 cups sugar to each 2 cups quince juice
juice of 1 lemon
½ cup boiling water

Boil peel and cores, strain and make up to 2 cups with hot water.
Make a syrup with this liquid and sugar as above.
Add quinces. Boil for about 2 hours, or until it will set when tested.
Add lemon juice and the boiling water before taking up.
Should be a fine red colour.

QUINCE & PINEAPPLE HONEY

2 cups water
12 cups sugar
5 large quinces, peeled and minced

1 large pineapple, peeled, hard core removed, and minced

Boil water and sugar for 10 minutes. Add fruit to the syrup.
Boil for 30 minutes or until will set. Do not over boil.
This is a golden-coloured jam.

QUINCE JAM

quinces
1 cup sugar to each 1 cup chopped quinces

Wipe quinces. Peel, core and cut into quarters.
Put peels and cores in pot, just cover with water, bring to boil.
    Boil gently till pale pink.
Cut fruit into small pieces. Sprinkle quinces with sugar and
    leave overnight.
Put in a pan with the water that the skins and cores were
    boiled in.
Do not add more sugar or water. Boil hard for about 1 hour.
Then boil gently until nice and red, and will set.

QUINCE JELLY

>quinces, cut fairly small (including cores and skins)
>1 cup warmed sugar to each 1 cup juice

Barely cover quinces, skins and cores with water.
Bring to the boil and simmer until it is a thick, soft pulp. Strain through a cloth overnight.
Sugar can be warmed in a meat dish in the oven. Bring juice to the boil and add sugar gradually.
Stir continually over a moderate heat until sugar is dissolved.
Bring to the boil again, and boil very fast at a rolling boil, until it will set when tested.

QUINCE & TOMATO JAM

>900g quinces, peeled, cored and minced, catching every drop of juice
>1.4kg ripe tomatoes, skinned and cut up roughly
>2.25kg sugar

Put quinces and tomatoes in a preserving pan and heat.
When hot, add sugar, stirring until dissolved.
Boil until jam is cooked and will set when tested.
Tastes like rich raspberry jam.

RASPBERRY OR STRAWBERRY JAM (3 Minute)

>raspberries or strawberries
>2 cups sugar to each 2 cups fruit when boiled

Bring berries to the boil. Add sugar and boil hard for only 3 minutes.
Retains bright colour and natural flavour.

RASPBERRY & RED CURRANT JAM

>raspberries and red currants
>1 cup sugar to each 1 cup cooked fruit

Pick over fruit and wash very gently. Do not leave in the water.
Drain, and put in a preserving pan. Crush a little fruit to start the juice.
Bring to the boil quickly. Add sugar.
When dissolved, boil rapidly until it will set, about 8 to 10 minutes.
Red currants may be strained before adding sugar.

RASPBERRY & RHUBARB JAM

2.7kg rhubarb, cut up small
3.6kg sugar
1.8kg raspberries

Sprinkle rhubarb with sugar and leave overnight.
Bring to the boil and cook until soft.
Add raspberries, and boil until it will set when tested.

RED CURRANT JELLY

4.5kg fruit
2 cups water
2 cups warmed sugar to
  each 2 cups juice
1 knob of butter
lemon juice (if desired)

Simmer fruit until soft. Strain through a jelly bag for 24 hours.
Add sugar. Bring to the boil and boil until it will set when tested.
Add butter. A little lemon juice is nice.

RHUBARB JAM

3.6kg rhubarb, cut into
  short pieces, with coarse
  parts of skin removed
340g sugar to each 450g fruit
900g tin strawberry or
  raspberry jam

Put rhubarb and sugar in a bowl and leave overnight.
Boil until jam sets when tested. Add tin of jam.

RHUBARB & LEMON JAM

rhubarb
450g sugar to each 450g rhubarb
juice and rind of 2 small lemons to each 1.8kg to 2.25kg rhubarb
1 walnut-sized knob of butter

Cut rhubarb into small pieces and cover with sugar. Leave overnight.
Add lemon juice and rind, and boil.
Boil for about 1 hour, or until it will set.
Drop in the butter before taking off the boil.
Rhubarb jam is always fairly liquid.

RHUBARB & PINEAPPLE JAM

1.8kg rhubarb
1 large tin pineapple, juice retained
1.4kg sugar

Cut up rhubarb and pineapple. Add sugar and leave overnight.
Next day, boil until it will set when tested.
Just before bottling, add the pineapple juice and stir well.
Bottle in usual way. A lovely pink colour.

ROSEHIP JAM

Hips are red fruits or seed pods which form when wild rose blooms have dried off. Make jam same day they are gathered. Work with all stainless steel utensils.

rosehips
2½ cups water to each 900g rosehips

1 cup sugar to each 2 cups purée
sugar to add when jam is made

Add water to rosehips and boil until tender.
Strain through a fine sieve, then through a double thickness of butter muslin to remove sharp hairs on seeds.
Add sugar and stir until thoroughly mixed and smooth.
Bring to simmer carefully and cook 10 minutes. Put into jam jars.
When cold, put a layer of sugar on top to help keep the flavour.

STRAWBERRY CONSERVE

2.7kg strawberries
2.7kg sugar

3 cups red currant juice or gooseberry juice

Put strawberries in a basin and sprinkle with half the sugar. Leave overnight.
Put currant or gooseberry juice in a pan with the remaining sugar and juice from the strawberries.
Boil for 8 to 10 minutes, stirring all the time.
Add strawberries and boil until set, about 20 minutes.
Skim. Fill warm jars. Cover when cold.
Whole strawberries in a heavy jelly.

STRAWBERRY JAM

1.8kg strawberries
juice of 4 lemons
1.8kg sugar

Cook fruit and lemon juice, simmering gently until soft.
Add sugar and stir until dissolved. Boil until it sets when tested.
Pot when half cold. Stir before bottling.

STRAWBERRY & GOOSEBERRY JAM

2.25kg gooseberries
7 cups water
4kg sugar
900g strawberries

Boil gooseberries in the water for 20 minutes.
Add sugar and stir until dissolved.
Add strawberries and boil for 45 minutes, or until it will set when tested.

STRAWBERRY & RHUBARB JAM

220g rhubarb
450g strawberries
680g sugar

Cut rhubarb to the size of a strawberry.
Cover rhubarb and strawberries with half the sugar. Leave overnight.
Next day, bring to the boil. Add remaining sugar and boil until it will jell.

TAMARILLO JAM

1.4kg tamarillos
450g green apples, peeled and minced
2 teacups water
1.8kg sugar
juice of 1 or 2 lemons

Scald tamarillos to peel. Cut up. Put apples in a pan with tamarillos and the water.
Bring to the boil. Add sugar, and boil until it will set, about 1 hour.
Add lemon juice, and bottle hot.

THREE FRUIT JELLY

900g black currants
900g red currants
450g raspberries

1 cup sugar to each
1 cup juice

Put fruit in a pan with just enough water to cover.
Bring slowly to the boil. Simmer gently until thoroughly cooked.
Put in a jelly bag and leave to drip overnight.
Next day, add sugar, dissolve and bring quickly to the boil.
Boil slowly for 15 minutes, or until it will set.

TOMATO & APPLE JAM

2.25kg ripe tomatoes
2.25kg apples, peeled, cored and cut up

450g preserved ginger, cut up
3.6kg sugar

Crush tomatoes in a preserving pan. Boil with other ingredients for 30 minutes.
Add sugar and stir until dissolved. Boil 1 hour on a low heat, until it sets.
No water needed.

TOMATO & PASSIONFRUIT JAM

1.8kg ripe tomatoes
1½ cups passionfruit pulp
2.25kg sugar

Skin tomatoes. Boil half the passionfruit skins until inside is soft. Scoop them out with a spoon. Add this pulp to tomatoes and passionfruit pulp.
Add sugar and stir until dissolved. Boil together until it will set when tested.

TOMATO & PINEAPPLE JAM

2 large pineapples
2.25kg tomatoes
sugar (340g for every 450g fruit pulp)

Peel and cut up pineapples. Skin and cut up tomatoes.
Boil pineapple and tomatoes together until pineapple is soft.
Add sugar to mixture, stirring frequently, for about 30 minutes or until mixture sets.
Remove hard core of pineapple.

GREEN TOMATO JAM (with Apples)

2.7kg green tomatoes, cut up
900g apples, cut up
225g preserved ginger, cut up
1 cup water
3.6kg sugar

Put fruit and ginger in pan with water. Boil, stirring frequently, for about 30 minutes.
Add sugar and stir until dissolved. Boil until it will set.

GREEN TOMATO JAM (with Lemon Juice)

1.4kg green tomatoes
juice of 6 lemons
115g shredded preserved ginger
1.8kg sugar

Slice tomatoes. Add lemon juice, ginger, and very little water to prevent sticking.
Boil for 30 minutes until soft. Add sugar and boil until will set when tested, about 45 minutes.

Preserving

Two main points are essential in successful preserving:

1. Sufficient processing or cooking at sufficiently high temperature to kill all bacteria, moulds and yeasts.

2. Complete sealing so that no air can get into jars afterwards. If fruits go mouldy, or ferment, while the seal appears to be airtight, it must be because the fruit was too ripe when preserved, or not sufficiently cooked, or the jars were not properly sterilised. If using open-pan (or stewing method), each jar must be taken one at a time from a hot oven, or hot water, filled right to the top, and sealed immediately, before any air has time to get in. Run a hot knife round the side of the filled jar very quickly to make sure no air bubbles have been trapped among the fruit. Store jars in a cool, dry, dark place.

Enzymes are the substances in all fresh fruit and vegetables which cause normal ripening. If the ripening process is not checked, it will go on until decay sets in. Extreme heat will check the growth of enzymes, as in preserving, or extreme cold, as in deep freezing.

Fermentation sometimes occurs in jars of preserved fruit. The seal may not be perfect or air bubbles may have been trapped among the fruit when filling the jars, or air might have got inside in some other way. Or the jars may have been stored in too warm a place. Fermentation causes a gas to be produced which forces loose the seals on the jars.

Acid foods are fruits, including tomatoes and rhubarb. They are processed safely at boiling point.

Non-acid foods are vegetables, meat and fish. These must be processed at a higher temperature than boiling point, and should be done in a pressure canner by applying 4.5kg to 6.75kg of steam

Preserved Beans, page 125

Preserved Beetroot (1), page 126

pressure. If non-acid foods are processed in a water-bath, they need 3 to 4 hours at boiling point, and even then should be boiled for 10 to 15 minutes before using or even tasting.

Preserve only good fruit just ripe. Damaged or bruised fruit can be cut and the good parts used for pulping.

THE STEWING METHOD
This is easy, and safe for fruit only.

Make a syrup using 2 cups water to each cup sugar — or less sugar if desired.
Boil sugar and water, and stir, over a low heat, until sugar is dissolved. Boil for 5 minutes.
Prepare the fruit — whole, halved, or sliced.
Drop fruit into boiling syrup and cook gently until soft but not mushy.
Have jars hot and sterilised. Have a board ready beside the boiling pan of fruit, and put one hot jar at a time on the board.
Fill quickly with fruit, using a perforated spoon (also hot and sterilised), cover with the syrup right up to overflowing and seal.
Stand out of draught and test after 24 hours according to directions given with the seal.
The pan of fruit must be kept boiling gently all the time you are bottling.
Store in a dry, cool, dark place. The jars may be wrapped round with brown paper to keep them dark.

WATER-BATH METHOD (For Acid Foods Only)
This is very easy and safe.

Pack the prepared fruit into clean jars.

Fill up to neck of jar with syrup (or water, but the syrup gives the fruit a much better flavour).

Cover with whatever type of seal you are using, according to the directions.

Place the jars on a rack (or folded cloths) in a deep pan and completely cover with cold water.

Bring slowly to simmering point, taking 1½ hours to do this. It is this slow heating that results in all bacteria, moulds and yeasts being killed throughout the whole of the contents of each jar; it also keeps the fruit a good colour and shape.

Maintain the boiling for 10 to 15 minutes for most fruits, but 30 minutes for pears and tomatoes. Lift out of water and cool on a wooden surface, out of draughts.

To save time you can pack the fruit into hot jars, cover with hot syrup, and lower the jars gently into a hot water-bath. Use the method as above. The processing time is shorter.

THE OVEN METHOD
Only fruits and tomatoes may be preserved in the oven. Many people object to this method because jars have been known to burst.

Have hot, sterilised jars, fill with the prepared fruit (whole or halved or sliced), put in very little liquid, and in the case of strawberries and raspberries no liquid at all is necessary; cover loosely with a patty pan or saucer or something similar.

Have oven at 120°C, and leave for 45 minutes to 1 hour until the fruit shrinks and is partly cooked. Tomatoes and pears generally need 30 minutes longer.

If the fruit has shrunk very much (as berries and rhubarb do), you can fill up the jars from 1 or 2 of the others, but return them to the oven again for a few minutes.

Have ready a saucepan of boiling syrup (or kettle of boiling water), take out one jar at a time, fill quite full with boiling syrup and seal immediately.

Stand on a wooden surface out of draughts.

This method is popular because you can process a few kilograms of fruit at any time without any trouble. Especially good for tomatoes and berries.

PULPING FRUIT (No Sugar)

This is an excellent way for preserving fruit ready for making into jam, or sauce, or for use in pies and tarts later on. By pulping it is preserved until you need it, and you can make up a little at a time.

Simply boil the fruit until soft and pulpy, using only enough water to prevent the fruit from burning.

Soft berry fruit and tomatoes should be crushed against the sides of the pan to draw sufficient juice to commence cooking, and no water will be needed at all.

For tomatoes, boil up again after straining, for 10 minutes. Harder fruits will need a little water, according to the kind.

When all is pulpy, have ready hot sterilised jars and take up one at a time to fill to overflowing with the boiling pulp, sealing each one immediately, before any air can get in.

When making into jam, bring pulp to boil, add cup for cup of sugar, stir until dissolved, and boil fast until jam will set when tested.

Less perfect, or even bruised fruit can be used for pulping, provided it is not over-ripe, and the bruised or damaged parts are cut away.

PRESERVING NON-ACID FOODS
(Vegetables, Meat, Fish)

Vegetables are safest if preserved by pressure-cooking. The makers of pressure cookers and pressure saucepans also often supply their own instructions for preserving. Non-acid foods, if not preserved under pressure, can only be done safely in a water-bath. Even then, they should be boiled for 15 minutes before using or even tasting.

BLANCHING

All vegetables should first be blanched — to clean the surface properly, to make them flexible so that they pack better, to reduce the loss of vitamin C, and to help the heat penetrate better during the processing.

The easiest way is to put the peas (or other vegetables) into a piece of butter muslin, plunge into boiling water for 3 to 5 minutes, then into cold water for 1 minute to make them easy to handle.

Vegetables need a little salt — 1 teaspoon to a 1 litre jar. A little sugar and vinegar may also be added to peas, beans, beetroot, corn and tomatoes.

APPLES (Cloved)

1.8kg apples
1.6kg sugar
2 cups water
12 cloves

Peel and core apples and divide into quarters.
Boil sugar, water and cloves to a syrup.
Add apples and bring to the boil.
Simmer gently until all the apple is cooked but not broken.
Lift out carefully into small hot jars. Seal immediately.
If done properly they should keep well, and are delicious with cold meat, cheese or salad.

PRESERVING BEANS BY SALT & SUGAR METHOD

To 1.2kg beans allow 2 cups salt and 1 cup sugar.
Cut beans as for the table and put in a bowl.
Mix sugar and salt well, sprinkle over and through beans, and leave overnight.
Next day, pack jars, cover with the brine which formed.
Keep in a cool place. Do not screw airtight.
Wash and cook as usual.

PRESERVED BEETROOT (1)

Peel and dice the beetroot.
Cook in boiling salted water until tender.
Take equal portions of vinegar and the liquid that the beet was boiled in.
Bring to the boil and pour over the beet in jars. Overflow and seal down.
This keeps very well and is like fresh cooked beet.

PRESERVED BEETROOT (2)

Three-parts cook beet, then dip in cold water and rub off skins.
Slice beet and pack at once into hot containers.
Add 1 teaspoon salt (not iodised) to each 1 litre jar.
Fill with fresh boiling water and sterilise 1 hour after adjusting lids. Or if done under pressure, 30 minutes to 4.5kg pressure.

BEETROOT (Spiced)

Cook beetroot in the usual way. Skin and slice into preserving jars. Make a spiced vinegar as follows:

4 cups water	8 cloves
15g peppercorns	30g sugar

Bring to the boil for a few minutes, pour over beetroot in jars, and close down immediately.

BERRY JUICE — OR JUICE OF ANY SOFT FRUIT

Crush fruits and allow to stand a little.
Add very little water, and place on the warm part of the stove to make juices flow.
Remove and strain through a cloth.
Bring to the boil. Add 115g sugar to each 2 cups juice.
Boil steadily for 5 minutes then strain through muslin.
Pour into sterilised bottles while boiling hot and put 1 teaspoon olive oil on top of each bottle.
Put in corks tightly. To use, soak up oil with cotton wool.

CANDIED CHERRIES

Make a very heavy syrup in the proportions of 450g sugar to 1 teacup of water.
Let it simmer until the sugar is dissolved.
Put cherries into the boiling syrup, and simmer very slowly until quite clear.
Pour off syrup, place fruit on flat dishes, and let dry in the sun or slow oven.
Will take several hours. When thoroughly dry, dust over with sugar, and store in paper-lined tins.

CANDIED VIOLETS & ROSE PETALS

Wash and rinse the flowers. Drain and spread out to dry.

Make a syrup of 2 cups sugar and ½ cup boiling water.

Stir constantly over a gentle heat until it reaches boiling point. Then stir in ⅛ teaspoon cream of tartar.

Allow to cook rapidly undisturbed until the 'soft ball' stage, tested by dropping a little syrup into cold water. It should be taken up and formed into a soft ball between thumb and forefinger.

Add flowers to boiling syrup, press them well under, and let it boil up once.

Pour gently, without shaking, into a meat platter rinsed in cold water, and leave to stand until next day.

Drain flowers from syrup, add another 1 cup of sugar to the syrup, and again bring to the soft ball stage.

Add flowers again, and leave until next day.

Repeat the process once more, and after the pot is removed from the heat, stir until the sugar turns grainy.

Separate flowers, and dust off any superfluous sugar.

Pack into boxes between sheets of waxed paper.

CANDIED PEEL

Cut citrus skin into quarters and soak in salt and water for 4 days.
Drain and boil in fresh water until tender.
Make syrup with 1 cup sugar and 1 cup water. Put peel into this and boil until soft.
Leave until next day. Remove peel and add to syrup the juice of 1 lemon and 1 cup sugar.
Boil until thick. Pour over peel, and gradually dry off in oven.
Orange peel is very nice done this way.

TO CRYSTALLISE FRUIT

Make a syrup with 450g sugar and 1 cup water.
Stir until dissolved, and when just at boiling point add ¼ teaspoon cream of tartar.
Leave off stirring, and allow to boil quickly for 3 to 4 minutes.
Test syrup by dropping a little into cold water — if it forms a soft ball between thumb and forefinger, it has reached desired stage.
Drop in fruit to be crystallised, a few at a time.
Lift out gently, and drain free from syrup. Place fruit on wire cake trays, and put in sun to dry.
When dry, make syrup as before, and when at 'soft ball' stage drop in fruit.
Put on wire trays, sift over coarse granulated sugar, and leave again in sun to dry.
When dry, pack in boxes between sheets of waxed paper. Keep in a cool, dry place.

FIGS, TO DRY

Make a strong syrup in the proportion of 450g sugar to 2 cups water.
When boiling, drop in whole figs and boil gently for 30 minutes, or until the fruit becomes clear.
Enough citric acid to cover half a ten cent piece may be added if the intense sweetness is not liked.
Drain clear figs and dry outdoors in the usual way. If conditions are dusty or the sun not strong enough, use a warm oven. Leave door ajar.
When dry, but still quite pliable, pack fruit in paper-lined boxes or airtight jars.
Spread ripe figs in a netting frame in the sun and leave to dry.
The air must be able to circulate freely all round them. When dry, store in boxes.

PICKLING FISH

Scale and clean fish and cut into fillets.
Pack into mason jars not too tight. Cover with vinegar, 1 teaspoon salt and a little pepper.
Screw down top lightly and process in boiling water for 2 to 3 hours.
Lift out and fill to the top with boiling vinegar. Screw down until airtight.
Oysters may be done in the same way, only sterilise 1 hour.
Crayfish also — cook crayfish first and take out of the shell; put in jars and cover with vinegar and sterilise 1 hour.

Candied peel, page 129

Mushrooms – Preserved, page 137

GRAPE JUICE

1 cup grapes (170g)
1 cup sugar
boiling water

Thoroughly clean a 1 litre jar (preferably with glass top).
Wash grapes, put into the jar and add sugar.
Fill jar with boiling water and close tightly.
The juice is ready for use in 6 weeks.

PRESERVED GRAPES

Take all fruit off stalks and pack in clean jars.
Stand jars in a warm oven and slowly increase the heat to about 180°C.
Cook until they change colour, then remove from oven, and re-fill jars, making 2 full ones out of 3 (when cooked they sink down).
Have your syrup boiling, overflow the jars and seal in the usual way.

PRESERVED GUAVAS

Make a syrup of 1 cup sugar to 2 cups water.
Wipe guavas and pack them in jars.
Cover with hot syrup and adjust lids according to their type.
Process the jars in a boiling water-bath for 15 minutes for 500ml jars and 25 minutes for 1 litre jars.
Leave jars to stand and then test the seals.

LEMONS, TO PRESERVE

Take large, firm lemons, and run a thread through the hard nib at the end of the lemon.
Tie ends of the string, and hang in a dry, airy place.
Do not let lemons touch each other, or anything else.
Put a layer of sand in a box. Lay clean lemons in a row, not touching each other.
Cover with more clean sand and continue layers until the box is full.
Keep in a cool place.

TO PRESERVE LEMON JUICE

Strain pure uncooked juice into small sterilised bottles, nearly filling the bottle.
Fill remaining space with olive oil, which excludes the air. Cork.
Keep in a cool place. When needed, drain off oil with cotton wool.

MEATS — TO KEEP

Bacon, to Cure, in One Week

To every 11.25kg meat use:

670g salt	220g brown sugar
110g pepper	30g saltpetre.

Mix dry ingredients well and divide into 3 parts.
Take 1 part daily for 3 days, heat in the oven as hot as the hand can bear, and rub both sides of the meat vigorously, keeping the mixture hot.
Turn meat daily, take out on the eighth day.
Rinse in warm water and hang to dry.
Hams may be left 2 days longer.

Bacon, to Cure

3.5kg coarse salt
1.4kg sugar
1 heaped teaspoon saltpetre
1 heaped teaspoon bicarbonate of soda
1 heaped tablespoon mace
1 tablespoon pepper

Mix well together. Sprinkle over bacon evenly, and leave to cure for 14 days, turning often.
Wash, swish with vinegar, and hang up.

Beef Pickle (1)

670g common salt
80g saltpetre
1 teaspoon black pepper
1.8kg brown sugar

Mix all together and rub over beef.
Rub and turn every day.

Beef Pickle (2)

560g common salt
450g coarse brown sugar
60g saltpetre
4 cups water

Boil all ingredients in the water for 10 minutes.
When cold, pour over meat.
Turn every day for a week.

Mutton, Ham, to Cure

For 1 hind-quarter of mutton, take:

    450g salt   1 grated nutmeg
    170g brown sugar   15g pepper
    30g saltpetre

Cut mutton into shape of a ham.
Mix other ingredients and rub well into the ham every day until the mixture is rubbed in.
Then press with a heavy weight. Let it lie about 14 days, turning every 3 days, and rubbing well with the pickle.
Take it out, let it drain, and hang up.
If you have the means for smoking it, do so.
When wanted to boil, soak for a few hours in water.
Put in cold water and boil for about 2 hours after it comes to the boil.

Mutton, to Pickle

Pour boiling water over common salt, about 2 litres to 450g salt.
Stir until dissolved. Leave until cold, and see if it will float a potato.
Add 2 or 3 tablespoons sugar to the brine.
Mutton can be kept in this for a week or two.

Mutton, Spiced Shoulder (Boned)

110g coarse brown sugar
1 dessertspoon powdered cloves
1 teaspoon pepper
1 teaspoon ground mace
1 salt spoon ground ginger
80g salt

Mix all but the salt, and rub into the shoulder.
Next day, rub in the salt.
Turn twice a day, and rub occasionally with the mixture for 8 or 9 days. Then roll up and tie.

Tongues, Pickle

2.7kg salt
900g sugar
12 litres water
80g saltpetre

Put this on the cooktop, stirring occasionally, and skim when it begins to boil.
Boil for at least 30 minutes. Strain into a tub, and let cool.
Add tongues.
A fortnight is the average time for pickling, or longer or shorter time according to the size and saltiness required.

MUSHROOMS — PRESERVED

If possible, preserve on the day they are picked — in any case, not longer than the following day.
Peel and place in a pot or preserving pan. Sprinkle each layer lightly with salt.
When juice flows, put over a gentle heat, stirring occasionally with a wooden spoon.
When sufficient juice is there, increase the heat and boil until cooked.
Turn into a basin, and when cool pack firmly into jars.
Fill with their own juice to within 12mm of the top. Seal.
Put in a water-bath and sterilise at boiling point for 2 hours.
Take out, and store.
If there is more juice than needed for the jars, add mace, peppercorns, salt and ginger to taste. Boil for 30 minutes, and thus make ketchup.

PRESERVED PASSIONFRUIT (1)

Allow ¾ cup sugar to each 1 cup passionfruit pulp.
Mix and put aside for 24 hours, stirring frequently until sugar dissolves, and to remove air bubbles.
Cork down. Use small jars.

PRESERVED PASSIONFRUIT (2)

One cup passionfruit pulp
1 cup sugar or honey

Bring to boiling point. Bottle in sterilised bottles and cork. Cool a little and dip in wax.

Less sugar may be used, in which case the pulp and sugar should be boiled for 1 to 2 minutes, then filled into sterilised bottles.

TOMATO PURÉE

Have good tomatoes, not over-ripe and bursting.

Cut up into a can (which may be lightly buttered).

Add no water, but a little salt (say 2 teaspoons for every 1.8kg to 2.25kg tomatoes), and a few peppercorns.

Bring slowly to the boil, stirring gently. Cook until soft and thick.

Strain through a sieve to remove seeds and skins.

Bring back to the boil for 8 to 10 minutes.

Fill sterilised jars to overflowing, sealing each one immediately as you work, so each is sealed while boiling.

Many cooks add 1 tablespoon sugar as well as the salt when cooking — not enough to sweeten but it does enhance the flavour.

TO PRESERVE TROUT

Skin and fillet trout. Cut into suitably sized pieces and sprinkle with salt and a little sugar.
Pack into jars with a generous lump of butter to each jar. No moisture. (The butter makes a covering for fish when cooked.)
Stand jars in a vessel of water and sterilise as for fruit.
Screw lids on tightly as soon as cooked, and leave to cool in vessel.
Next day sterilise again without loosening the lids. Cool again in the vessel.
Tighten lids as much as possible. Use new rubbers always.
Excellent. Tastes like salmon.

HOW TO PRESERVE A HUSBAND

Be careful in your selection. Do not choose too young. When once selected, give your entire thoughts to preparation for domestic use. Some insist on keeping them in a pickle, others are constantly getting them into hot water. This may make them sour, hard and sometimes bitter. Even poor varieties may be made sweet, tender and good by garnishing them with patience, well-sweetened with love and seasoned with kisses. Wrap them in a mantle of charity. Keep warm with a steady fire of domestic devotion and serve with peaches and cream. Thus prepared, they will keep for years.

RECIPE INDEX

apple
    Apple Chutney 21
    Apples (Cloved) 125
    Apple Jelly 68
    Blackberry & Apple Jelly 72
    Elderberry & Apple Jam 78
    Feijoa, Guava & Apple Jelly 79
    Fruit Chutney (with Quinces) 26
    Fruit Salad Jam (Fresh) (2) 81
    Green Tomato Jam (with Apples) 117
    Japonica & Apple Jelly 86
    Laurel Berry & Apple Jam 87
    Mint & Apple Chutney 28
    Mint & Apple Jelly 95
    Passionfruit & Apple Jam 98
    Tomato & Apple Jam 115
    Worcestershire Sauce 63
apricot
    Apricot Chutney 21
    Apricot Ginger 69
    Apricot Jam (Fresh) 71
    Apricot & Lemon Jam 69
    Apricot & Orange Jam 70
    Apricot & Pineapple Jam 70
    Fruit Salad Jam (Fresh) (1) 81
    Fruit Salad Jam (Fresh) (2) 81
Bacon, To Cure 133–34
beans
    Bean Relish 22
    Choko Pickle 42
    Chow Chow 24
    Mother's Pickle 46
    Piccalilli 30
    Preserving Beans 125
    Sweet Piccalilli 30
Beef Pickle (1) 134
Beef Pickle (2) 134
beetroot
    Beetroot Chutney 22
    Beetroot Relish (Uncooked) 23
    Beetroot (Spiced) 126
    Preserved Beetroot (1) 126
    Preserved Beetroot (2) 126
Berry Juice 127
black currants
    Black Currant Jam (1) 74
    Black Currant Jam (2) 74
    Five-Minute Berry Jam 80
    Plum & Black Currant Jam 104
    Three Fruit Jelly 115
blackberry
    Blackberry & Apple Jelly 72
    Blackberry & Crab Apple Jelly 72
    Blackberry & Elderberry Jam 73
    Blackberry Jam 71
    Blackberry & Plum Jam 73
    Blackberry Pickle 38
Bright Red Pure Tomato Sauce 62
cabbage
    Cabbage Pickle (Uncooked) 38
    Cabbage Pickle (White) 39
    Mixed Pickle 46
    Mother's Pickle 46
    Red Cabbage Pickle 39
Candied Peel 129
Candied Violets & Rose Petals 128

Cape Gooseberry & Lemon Jam 75
Cape Gooseberry Jam 74
Capers, Pickled 40
cauliflower
   Cauliflower Pickle 40
   Cauliflower & Pineapple Pickle 41
   Mixed Pickle 46
   Mother's Pickle 46
   Piccalilli 30
   Sweet Mustard Pickle 48
   Sweet Piccalilli 30
Celery Pickles (with Tamarillos) 42
cherry
   Candied Cherries 127
   Cherry & Red Currant Jam 75
choko
   Choko Chutney 23
   Choko & Passionfruit Jam 76
   Choko Pickle 42
Chow Chow 24
crab apple & blackberry jelly 72
Cranberry Jelly 76
cucumber
   Chow Chow 24
   Cucumber Pickles (Small) 43
   Cucumber Relish 25
   Mixed Pickle 46
   Mother's Pickle 46
   Pickled Cucumbers (Jewish Method) 43
   Sweet Mustard Pickle 48
   Sweet Piccalilli 30
   Sweet Pickled Cucumbers 44
Damson Jam 77
Dried Peach Jam 100
Economy Pickle 44
elderberry
   Elderberry & Apple Jam 78
   Elderberry Jelly 77
Feijoa, Guava & Apple Jelly 79
Feijoa Jam 78

fig
   Economy Pickle 44
   Fig Chutney 25
   Fig Conserve (Fresh) 79
   Fig Jam (Fresh) 80
   Figs, To Dry 130
fish
   Pickling Fish 130
   To Preserve Trout 139
Five-Minute Berry Jam 80
Fruit Chutney (with Quinces) 26
Fruit Salad Jam (Fresh) (1) 81
Fruit Salad Jam (Fresh) (2) 81
gherkins, pickled 45
gooseberry
   Five-Minute Berry Jam 80
   Gooseberry Jam 82
   Gooseberry Mint Jelly 82
   Green Gooseberry & Cherry Plum Jam 83
   Green Gooseberry Chutney 26
   Green Gooseberry Marmalade 84
   Indian Chutney (with Gooseberry) 27
grape
   Grape Jelly 83
   Grape Juice 131
   Green Grape Jam 84
   Preserved Grapes 131
Green Gooseberry & Cherry Plum Jam 83
Green Gooseberry Chutney 26
Green Gooseberry Marmalade 84
Green Grape Jam 84
Green Tomato Chutney 35
Green Tomato Jam (with Apples) 117
Green Tomato Jam (with Lemon Juice) 117
Green Tomato Pickle 53
Green Tomato Sauce 63
guava
   Feijoa, Guava & Apple Jelly 79

Guava Jelly 85
Preserved Guavas 132
Hawthorn Jelly 85
Indian Chutney (with Gooseberry) 27
Japonica & Apple Jelly 86
Japonica Jelly 86
Kiwifruit & Orange Jam 88
Kiwifruit Jam 87
Laurel Berry & Apple Jam 87
lemon
    Apricot & Lemon Jam 69
    Cape Gooseberry & Lemon Jam 75
    Green Tomato Jam (with Lemon Juice) 117
    Lemons, To Preserve 132
    Pear Ginger (with Lemon Juice) 102
    Rhubarb & Lemon Jam 111
    To Preserve Lemon Juice 133
loganberry
    Five-Minute Berry Jam 80
    Loganberry Jam 88
    Loganberry & Plum Jam 88
Mango Chutney 27
marmalade
    Dundee 89
    Easy 89
    Green Gooseberry 84
    NZ Grapefruit (Johnny's) 90
    Prize 90
    With Green Tomatoes 91
marrow
    Marrow Jam 91
    Marrow & Quince Jam 92
    Piccalilli 30
meat
    Bacon, To Cure 133–34
    Beef Pickle (1) 134
    Beef Pickle (2) 134
    Mutton, Ham, To Cure 135
    Mutton, Spiced Shoulder (Boned) 136
    Mutton, To Pickle 135
Tongues, Pickle 136
Medlar Jam 92
melon
    Melon Jam 93
    Melon & Passionfruit Jam 94
    Melon & Tamarillo Jam 94
mint
    Gooseberry Mint Jelly 82
    Mint & Apple Chutney 28
    Mint & Apple Jelly 95
    Mint Sauce (Preserved) 58
Mixed Pickle 46
Mock Raspberry Jam (or Strawberry) 95
Mother's Pickle 46
Mulberry Jam 96
mushroom
    Mushroom Ketchup (1) 58
    Mushroom Ketchup (2) 59
    Mushrooms – Pickled 47
    Mushrooms – Preserved 137
Mutton, Ham, To Cure 135
Mutton, Spiced Shoulder (Boned) 136
Mutton, To Pickle 135
Nasturtium Seeds 48
Nectarine Jam 96
onion
    Chow Chow 24
    Mixed Pickle 46
    Pears (Pickled with Onion) 51
    Pickled Onions 49
    Pickled Onions with Honey 50
    Sweet Piccalilli 30
orange
    Apricot & Orange Jam 70
    Candied Peel 129
    Kiwifruit & Orange Jam 88
    Marmalade (Dundee) 89
    Marmalade (Easy) 89
    Parsley Jelly 97
passionfruit

Choko & Passionfruit Jam 76
Fruit Salad Jam (Fresh) (1) 81
Melon & Passionfruit Jam 94
Passionfruit & Apple Jam 98
Passionfruit Jam 97
Passionfruit & Tomato Jam 98
Peach & Passionfruit Jam 101
Pear & Passionfruit Jam 101
Preserved Passionfruit (1) 137
Preserved Passionfruit (2) 138
Tomato & Passionfruit Jam 116
peach
　Dried Peach Jam 100
　Fruit Salad Jam (Fresh) (1) 81
　Peach Chutney 28
　Peach Jam (1) 99
　Peach Jam (2) 99
　Peach Jam (3) 100
　Peach & Passionfruit Jam 101
　Peach & Plum Chutney 29
　Pickled Peaches 50
　Pineapple & Peach Jam 103
pear
　Fruit Salad Jam (Fresh) (2) 81
　Pear Ginger (with Lemon Juice) 102
　Pear & Passionfruit Jam 101
　Pears (Pickled with Onion) 51
Persimmon Jelly 102
Piccalilli 30
Pickled Cucumbers (Jewish
　Method) 43
Pickled Figs (Fresh) 45
Pickled Gherkins 45
Pickled Green Walnuts 55
Pickled Onions 49
Pickled Onions with Honey 50
Pickled Peaches 50
Pickled Shallots (1) 52
Pickled Shallots (2) 52
Pickling Fish 130
pineapple

Apricot & Pineapple Jam 70
Cauliflower & Pineapple Pickle 41
Fruit Salad Jam (Fresh) (1) 81
Pineapple & Peach Jam 103
Quince & Pineapple Honey 107
Rhubarb & Pineapple Jam 111
Tomato & Pineapple Jam 116
plum
　Blackberry & Plum Jam 73
　Damson Jam 77
　Fruit Salad Jam (Fresh) (2) 81
　Green Gooseberry & Cherry Plum
　　Jam 83
　Loganberry & Plum Jam 88
　Peach & Plum Chutney 29
　Plum & Black Currant Jam 104
　Plum Chutney 31
　Plum Jam 103
　Plum & Raspberry Jam 104
　Plum Sauce 60
Preserved Beetroot (1) 126
Preserved Beetroot (2) 126
Preserved Grapes 131
Preserved Guavas 132
Preserved Passionfruit (1) 137
Preserved Passionfruit (2) 138
Preserving Beans 125
Prune & Rhubarb Jam 105
Prune Pickle 51
Pumpkin Jam 105
Quick Chutney 32
quince
　Fruit Chutney (with Quinces) 26
　Marrow & Quince Jam 92
　Quince Chutney 32
　Quince Conserve 106
　Quince Honey 106
　Quince Jam 107
　Quince Jelly 108
　Quince & Pineapple Honey 107
　Quince & Tomato Jam 108

raspberry
- Mock Raspberry Jam
  (or Strawberry) 95
- Plum & Raspberry Jam 104
- Raspberry & Red Currant Jam 109
- Raspberry & Rhubarb Jam 110
- Raspberry or Strawberry Jam
  (3 Minute) 109
- Three Fruit Jelly 115

Red Cabbage Pickle 39

red currant
- Cherry & Red Currant Jam 75
- Five-Minute Berry Jam 80
- Raspberry & Red Currant Jam 109
- Red Currant Jelly 110
- Three Fruit Jelly 115

rhubarb
- Five-Minute Berry Jam 80
- Prune & Rhubarb Jam 105
- Raspberry & Rhubarb Jam 110
- Rhubarb Chutney 33
- Rhubarb Jam 110
- Rhubarb & Lemon Jam 111
- Rhubarb & Pineapple Jam 111
- Rhubarb Relish 33
- Strawberry & Rhubarb Jam 114

rose petals, candied 128

Rosehip Jam 112

shallots
- Pickled Shallots (1) 52
- Pickled Shallots (2) 52

strawberry]
- Five-Minute Berry Jam 80
- Mock Raspberry Jam
  (or Strawberry) 95
- Raspberry or Strawberry Jam
  (3 Minute) 109
- Strawberry Conserve 112
- Strawberry Jam 113
- Strawberry & Gooseberry Jam 113
- Strawberry & Rhubarb Jam 114

Sweet Mustard Pickle 48

Sweet Piccalilli 30

Sweet Pickled Cucumbers 44

tamarillo
- Celery Pickles (with Tamarillos) 42
- Melon & Tamarillo Jam 94
- Tamarillo Chutney 33
- Tamarillo Jam 114
- Tamarillo Sauce 60

Three Fruit Jelly 115

To Preserve Lemon Juice 133

To Preserve Trout 139

tomato
- Bright Red Pure Tomato Sauce 62
- Fruit Chutney (with Quinces) 26
- Green Tomato Chutney 35
- Green Tomato Jam
  (with Apples) 117
- Green Tomato Jam (with
  Lemon Juice) 117
- Green Tomato Pickle 53
- Green Tomato Sauce 63
- Mixed Pickle 46
- Passionfruit & Tomato Jam 98
- Quince & Tomato Jam 108
- Sweet Mustard Pickle 48
- Sweet Piccalilli 30
- Tomato & Apple Jam 115
- Tomato Chutney 34
- Tomato Ketchup 61
- Tomato & Passionfruit Jam 116
- Tomato & Pineapple Jam 116
- Tomato Purée 138
- Tomato Relish 34
- Tomato Sauce 61
- Tomato Sauce without Vinegar 62

Tongues, Pickle 136

Vinegar (Spiced) 53

violets, candied 128

walnuts
- Pickled Green Walnuts 55
- Walnuts (Sweet Pickled) 54

Worcestershire Sauce 63